The Native American Music Directory

3rd Edition
(Revised)

Compiled and Edited
by
Gregory Gombert

Music Café Publishing
Santa Fe, New Mexico

© 2004 Gregory Gombert

Originally published as:
A Guide to Native American Music Recordings
© 1994 Gregory Gombert

Music Café Publishing
Santa Fe, NM

Book design: Music Café Publishing

Cover art: Darren Johnston

ISBN 0-9644454-9-2

Gombert, Gregory
    Native American Music Directory / compiled an edited with notes by Gregory Gombert

1. Folk music – Discography
2. Indians of North America – Music – Discography

ML   2003

Acknowledgements

I wish to thank Canyon Record Productions, Indian House Records, Sunshine Records, Sweet Grass Records, Smithsonian / Folkways Recordings, and Arbor Records for their assistance.

Special thanks to Brandon Friesen and James Fortune.

Dedicated to my late parents, George and Gertrude Gombert and their granddaughters, Olivia Marlise Gombert and Kristin Marie Gombert.

Contents

Preface

This book began as an offshoot of two years of graduate research in ethnomusicology at Arizona State University and contact with record companies and the Native American community. The listed commercially available recordings represent Native American recordings from the United States, Canada, and Mexico.

This third edition builds on the success of the first two editions, and attempts to focus and meet the needs of the Native American music community, libraries, record companies, and the record buying public.

Changes in content have been made, in step with changes in current Native American music trends and a desire to preserve the traditional value of Native American music. While many Native American performers began following hybrid musical paths beginning in the 1980s, these performers are now well entrenched in standard music genres within the music industry at large, and show up in record bins at stores in the same manner, Therefore, performers who record in standardized music categories such as new age, jazz, blues, rock, rap, etc., are not included in this edition. I have focused, rather, on current trends within the Native community toward intertribalism, the recording of pow wow and other intertribal music styles, and the preservation of traditional Native American music commercially available recordings.

Intercultural understanding is of the utmost importance now and in the future. A solid understanding and appreciation of the differences among our cultures can only help prevent communication breakdown and potential human disaster. This book is presented to fulfill my belief that research should be available to the public as well as the halls of academia.

This book is dedicated to the souls we lost and heroes we found on September 11, 2001.

Gregory Gombert

Introduction

A History of Recording Native American Music

I. Background on music recording

The recording of Native American music began shortly after the invention of the phonograph by Thomas Alva Edison in 1877. Although the first version of this machine produced an aural record by means of a rigidly mounted stylus cutting "hill and dale" grooves onto tin foil cylinders, by 1877 wax coated cardboard cylinders were most preferred by recording personnel.

By 1889, thirty three U.S. companies had bought licenses to lease phonographs. Their initial income was generated by coin operated music machines. John Philip Sousa and the United States Marine Corps Band recorded favorite songs for public purchase from Columbia, while other musicians of high caliber in the 1890s, such as cornetist Jules Levy and tenor Ed Francis, were recorded and simply catalogued under general descriptive headings such as Sentimental, Topical, Comic, Irish, and Negro.

Early ethnomusicologists Otto Abraham and E.M. von Hornbostel wrote that the phonograph enabled one to "record a piece of music and study it at leisure I the studio, where attention is not so much distracted visually as it is at performances by exotic peoples." There is no doubt that the intellectual climate of the time encouraged early collectors to regard the recordings of songs as a process similar to the gathering of scientific specimens.

At the turn of the twentieth century, lands were taken from Indian people for the progress of a growing American nation, and Native Americans were commonly sent to boarding school and Christian churches-a forced adoption of the white man's ways. Ironically, at the same time these punishments were being delivered, a group of non-Indian researchers, with a deep interest in the preservation of ancient Indian ceremonial songs and languages, proceeded into the "field" to capture their music on wax cylinders via the phonograph.

A trend had begun with collectors like Jesse Walter Fewkes, Alice C. Cunningham, and Frances Densmore, to record Indian songs, analyze or describe them, catalogue the recordings, and store them for future reference. By the early 1900s, archival facilities had even been built where roughly 15,000 recordings could be contained. The main centers in the United States were the Archive of Folk Song at the Library of Congress in Washing, D.C., and the Archives of Folk and Primitive Music at Indiana University.

The introduction of the cleaner sounding 78 RPM gramophone by Emile Berliner in 1895 created the first great change in the recording environment. Since these machines were sold to the public mainly for playback purposes, the recording technician now owned a "master copy," representing a "product."

A second change occurred when the disc graphophone player appeared on the public market in 1902, a machine which could play back disc "pressing" (copies) of recordings, thereby creating a "sales market."

With these two changes in technology, an important philosophical split developed between the scientific world, which utilized cylinder recordings for study purposes, and a newly established "record industry," whose sole goal was disc copy sales.

Magnetic tape machines were introduced in 1947, and with them came an ease and portability that allowed Native American music enthusiasts to become professionals. Records could be made just about anywhere, as long as there was a pressing company available.

The 33 $^{1/3}$ RPM long playing disc arrived in 1948, and its capacity to hold longer segments of music paved the way for commercial record companies. Discs, which formerly could only hold one song per side, could now record several songs, and anthologies of Native American tribal music resulted.

Record labels presenting American Indian songs developed by the late 1940s, the two largest being American Indian Soundchiefs in Oklahoma, and Canyon Records in Arizona. Turn-of-the-century field recordings, made on phonograph cylinders, were also now made commercially available on LP discs by the Folkways label, a record division of the Smithsonian Institution, and the Library of Congress. Music styles recorded through the 1950s consisted of traditional tribal songs, pow wow songs, peyote songs of the Native American Church, and Indian gospel music.

The era of cassette recording began in the late 1960s, with 8 track cassettes (playback only) introduced first, and ¼ inch recordable cassettes by the mid 1970s. Tape recorders put control into the hands of the listener, and recordings could be duplicated and passed among music fans from different regions around the country. Although this also had happened years earlier with LPs, it was accelerated so that new intertribal songs and hybrid music forms developed and spread more rapidly.

During the decade of the sixties, Russell Moore was playing jazz trombone with Louis Armstrong's band, Tom Bee's group X.I.T. was pounding out its political Indian rock around the country, and Buffy Sainte-Marie was writing and performing her own brand of folk music as a sound stage for Native American rights. Native artists at this time were vocalizing the atrocities brought upon their culture groups, and demanding justice, in step with the general social chaos of the sixties.

In the 1970s, country western and gospel recordings gained popularity, keeping up sales with other current styles. This music demonstrates an increased blending of Indian culture with that of established white America, an ability to adapt and adjust by American Indian people.

Several new record companies began production of traditional music, along with intertribal styles, while the already established companies began exploring new Native music styles such as country western and rock. Intensified intertribal attitudes were reflected by the multitude of pow wow recordings made through the use of the cassette recorder by Indian performers themselves, to capture new songs and performances of various pow wow groups, as they performed around the country. Pow wows represent a time for Native people from differing culture backgrounds to get together and celebrate their "Indian-ness," separate from the greater American culture which they were forced to adapt to in both careers and education.

With the production of R. Carlos Nakai's synthesizer and flute cassette *Changes* in 1980, along with its distribution under the "new age" heading, a new non-Indian audience was added to the Native American music buying public.

This music style, perhaps more than any other, has built a bridge for Native American music to be purchased and appreciated by a non-Indian audience.

A host of new record companies sprang up to accommodate this market, including Sound of America Records, Silverwave Records, and Celestial harmonies, along with many smaller independent labels. Recordings in contemporary styles of new age, rock, rap, reggae, and rockabilly evolved into cleaner sounding, more meticulously produced compact discs, the preferred format for non-Indian listeners.

In the 1990s, the trend in American Indian music became swallowed up into a new "global music" market, and was categorized accordingly at record stores, along with African music, Latin music, and other music styles from around the globe. A liberal political climate in the United States created an interest and compassion for others around the world and, curiously, Native American music was dropped into this category.

New productions of previously unreleased traditional tribal music were released by companies like New World Records, Auvidis Unesco, Smithsonian/Folkways, and Indian House Records. Titles were usually available on both cassette and CD now, and copies of Library of Congress original cylinder recordings were now available on LP and cassette. Behind the glamour of high sales in "world music" and "new age" record bins however, the sale of intertribal pow wow music far surpassed these sales, but to the Native community primarily. We see here a footprint for the twenty first century and the attitudes toward Native American music and culture by non-Indians, as well as the increased strength of intertribal development by Native Americans.

The rich and diverse Native American recording environment of the 1990s, with its acceptance by non-Indian listeners and homogenization into the compassionate "global music" trends, has changed with the social climate in the United States.

American has become a country with an almost insurmountable chasm between rich and poor now, and as technology takes a bigger role than ever in our lives, many music styles which were developed here and are indeed American in heritage, are falling out of popularity for generic styles which are presented in the faces of television watchers and internet users. Native American music sales have fallen off with non-Indian buyers, much in the same way the American jazz music and classical music have. Another contributing factor has been a trend by younger music listeners in the U.S. to pirate songs they like in digital format from free internet web sites, rather than buying them on CDs or cassettes. We are left with an increasingly under educated music public in the United States, with tastes that grow more and more narrow as less options are presented to them via mass media.

The year 2001 saw the first official acceptance of Native American music by the general American audience. In 2001, the National Academy of Recording Arts and Sciences chose to debut a new category in the Grammy Folk awards category. The first Native American Category Grammy went to Tom Bee and Douglas Spotted Eagle, producers, for "Gathering of Nations Powwow," voted "Best Native American Recording."

Ironically, sales to a non-Indian audience were waning as the first Grammy was presented 2001, and the following awards in 2002 and 2003. However, sales continue strong within the Native American community, as an intertribal nation gets stronger every year within the larger nation of America.

Therefore, the Native American record industry is stronger now than ever, and the current artistic environment is rich and flourishing. Native American music in this century has become a healing community vehicle almost strictly for the Native American audience. Intertribal pow wow music sales are at an all time high, and new groups come onto the scene daily throughout the U.S. and Canada. We certainly can't categorize American Indian tribes as rich, but they are an inspiring example of poor cultures coming together to find strength among each other's tribes and heritages, while corporations, government, and mass media have a stranglehold on the masses around the world. Non-Indian people in America, splintered into small groups who cannot seem to cross boundaries and find sameness in each other, could learn a great deal from the intertribal strength of Native America.

II. Early Ethnographic Recording of American Indian Music

> The buffalo were disappearing, and as they did they said: "as we leave, your ways leave with us; but someday we will return and, when we do, these ways will return also - Blackfoot belief

> The U.S. government is a strange monster with many heads. One head doesn't know what the others are up to (Lame Deer 1979:209).

From Wounded Knee through World War II: Collecting songs from the "vanishing race"

The year 1890 was one of grave importance and sadness for American Indian peoples in the United States. On December 29th of that year the first torn and bleeding bodies of those men, women and children who had survived a butchering by U.S. soldiers at Wounded Knee, South Dakota were brought to an Episcopal mission at Pine Ridge to heal, with a banner reading "Peace on Earth Good Will to Men" hanging over the pulpit (Brown 1970:445). This massacre of nearly 300 Sioux people (Ibid.444) represented something greater according to Black Elk: "A people's dream died there...There is no center any longer, and the sacred tree is dead" (Neihardt 1932:230). Sioux spirit, echoing the sentiments of most American Indian peoples, was broken, and Indians were resigned to live their lives in a new manner brought on by the white man.

It is quite ironic that a keen interest in the traditions and customs of Indian peoples occurred within the U.S. Bureau of American Ethnology at the same time that other branches of the government, namely the Bureau of Indian Affairs and the U.S. Army, were hard at work blotting out Indian culture through assigning reservations, creating boarding schools, and other forced punishments (Debo 1970:278-288).

If Thomas Edison's vision for the use of his newly invented phonograph was one of integrity, as a tool for teaching languages and preserving great musical performances, music collectors of the 1890s viewed this tool with similar intent. Due to the relative permanency of cylinder recordings produced by this machine, they were eager to preserve the musical and linguistic heritage of American Indians, as these cultures caved in to a devastating assimilation process in the United States (Brady 1984:3).

In the same year that the Wounded Knee massacre took place, a zoologist named Jesse Walter Fewkes tested a phonograph in the field by recording Passamaquoddy Indian music in Maine. In 1890, Fewkes noted:

> "I found that songs and stories of these Indians can be written out from these records on the wax cylinders with a degree of accuracy which will, in the main, answer the purposes of the linguist. As these records may be preserved indefinitely, and may be repeated over and over again at the wish of the student, it is possible to study the music and words with great precision (Ibid.3)."

After the initial expeditions by Fewkes, a great number of explorations to Indian lands were conducted with the goal of preserving Indian music. Through the 1950s, some sponsoring institutions included the School of American Research, Columbia University, the American Museum of Natural History, and the Peabody Museum at Harvard (Ibid.4). By and large, the greatest amount of research was sponsored by the Bureau of American Ethnology, an institution established in 1879.

Some recordings received additional written documentation in the form of reports which analyzed the music, and one of the noted ethnographers to publish such studies during this time period was Alice Cunningham Fletcher. Sponsored by the Peabody Museum, she published a 152 page paper entitled "A Study of Omaha Music" in 1893. Ninety-two Omaha Indian songs were recorded by Fletcher and musical analysis was provided. From a contemporary viewpoint, one drawback to early reports like Fletcher's is the use of European art music terminology to examine the music, as seen in this excerpt from "A Study of Omaha Indian Music:"

> The most striking peculiarities of rhythm is the mixture of twos and threes in the same measure. The Mekasee Song, No. 58, has two examples represented by dotted quarters, while the song has three quarter notes in the measure. This is the same rhythm to be found in the No. 20 of the Mendelssohn "Song Without Word," in the "Abschied," Op. 82 Schumann and elsewhere in the works of the modern romantic composers (Fletcher 1893:53).

Another drawback to early studies like Fletcher's are the absence of documentation or description of any relevant cultural background for the music, such as ritual, dance, dress, instruments.

In the 1890s and early 1900s, Frances Densmore was the most prolific of the Bureau of American Ethnology's collectors of Indian music. However, she held a different view of her studies than simpler documentation in European terms. Densmore's heart, she claimed, was with the Indians, as she once wrote:

> I heard an Indian drum when I was very, very young, Others heard the same drum and the sound was soon forgotten, but I have followed it all these years. Unconsciously, it has called me, and I have followed it across the continent from British Columbia to the Everglades of Florida, over the plains and mountains, across the desert-always the Indian drum calling me (Hofman 1968:1).

Along with countless recordings and transcriptions, Densmore's reports for museums, historical societies and the Bureau of American Ethnology through the 1950s included detailed descriptions of events going on around her as she recorded. She viewed dance clothing, rituals, beliefs, music instruments, and the people themselves to be as important as catalogued recordings.

By the early 1900s, other researchers developed an interest in the preservation of American Indian music. Laura Bolton recorded a variety of Indian music, as part of her worldwide collecting of music and instruments. She produced excellent recordings on custom made equipment which utilized aluminum discs for sound storage, and a number of her recordings were released for publication later through the Smithsonian Folkways record label (Isaacs 1988:2). In the 1920s and 1930s, George Herzog and Helen H. Roberts began recording and studying American Indian music from an ethnomusicological perspective, and incorporated cultural description into their reports. Willard Rhodes also documented a great deal of music for the Bureau of Indian Affairs in the 1940s, and many of the recordings of these three scholars were published later by the Library of Congress and Smithsonian Folkways (Ibid).

By the late 1920s, research and recordings had accumulated to such a degree that archives for their storage were needed. In the field of musicology in Europe, the Phonogramm-Archiv in Berlin had bee4n used since 1900, and a similar need in the United States initiated the Archive of Folk Song at the Library of Congress in Washington, D.C. in 1928 (Shelemay 1991:282). This facility, along with various museums around the U.S., was representative of the need by the scholarly community to preserve recordings for the sake of future study. This body of countless recordings can be likened to the documentary Indian photographs of Edward Curtis, giving a colonial view in disjointed images of what Indian life is assumed to have been like before the arrival of the white man. Songs for recordings during the early 1900s were sung in the "old way," with singing styles and languages not used anymore by contemporary musicians (Scabby Robe 1993), and it should also be noted that performances were contrived and staged a good deal of the time (Brady 1984:21). Frances Densmore referred to a specific attraction to the Indian music of a bygone era which perhaps fulfilled a fantasy, based on the European Enlightenment, of an uncorrupted man in communion with nature:

> The purpose of the present work was to find and record the Indian songs that pertained to the old life and still survive in a tribe living under modern conditions, as the interest was not in modern Indian songs, composed within a generation, but in the old songs of the chiefs, warriors long dead, and the medicine-men who treated the sick and worked magic, the selection of a tribe or of tribes for this study became a matter of importance (Densmore 1936:13).

As early as 1893, with Fletcher's "A Study of Omaha Indian Music," we can see a strong need to categorize Indian songs from a Western viewpoint, a practice expanded upon later by ethnomusicologists. Her study groups Omaha songs into three categories: 1) Class songs-religious songs only sung by initiates, 2) Social songs-songs of certain secret societies, along with dance and game songs, and 3) Songs which relate to mystery, dreams, or the sweatlodge (Fletcher 1893:248). Ninety-two songs were recorded onto cylinders for this report, and all songs were transcribed and arranged in traditional European four part harmony. In "Cheyenne and Arapaho Music" (1936) by Frances Densmore, seventy-two songs are placed into ten designated categories and clearly labeled as to function, as they were recorded to cylinders for this Southwest Museum study.

In both Densmore's and Fletcher's studies of music, along with earlier reports of Fewkes in 1890, there were also linguistic observations, somewhat simplistic analyses of traits for the tribes being studied. Based on this early linguistic ethnography, anthropologists George Herzog (1928) and Helen H. Roberts (1936) began to develop "culture areas" for American Indians, based on shared traits. Ethnomusicologist Bruno Nettl would later (1954) link these traits through further study to arrive at six "music style areas" for American Indian music. However, as Leanne Hinton points out:

> The boundaries between areas are never exact (groups often will show characteristic of more than one culture area), nor can the correlation between linguistic, musical, or cultural studies ever be exact, because different sorts of traits have different sorts of diffusion patterns (1986:13).

Regardless of intent, a trend had begun to lump tribal traditions into large areas of similarity, with a possible result being a partial image of American Indian peoples and their music traditions, a weakened image of tribal identity.

Fieldworker-informant dynamics and U.S.-Indian relations

The U.S. government's relationship with American Indians from the turn of the century through the early 1900s was strained, to say the least. An evolving policy of control over the Indians was implemented through Bureau of Indian Affairs agents who were assigned to reorganize Indian governments so they could be more easily engulfed by U.S. procedure (Deloria 1984:28), and to develop boarding schools, along with Christian agents, thereby "civilizing" the Indians.

Although Alice C. Fletcher's success as a fieldworker among the Omaha and Osage peoples is attributed to her private generosity and courtesy toward them, including legislative activity on their behalf (Brady 1985:161), many fieldworkers reflected a U.S. policy of brutality and conquer. Matilda Cox Stevenson, an original Bureau of American Ethnology fieldworker, while working with the Zuni Indians of New Mexico, was a peculiarity in popular newspapers for "subduing a threatening 'savage' by beating him about the head with her umbrella" and for violating a no-photograph rule among the Zuni (Ibid.162). There appeared to be a zeal in fieldworkers' quest for information, along with the assumption that informants were brimming containers ready to be emptied of their knowledge. The goal was to retrieve as many cylinders as possible, to later evaluate the music out of context in a laboratory setting and, in Densmore's case, "the phonograph streamlined the operation to such an extent that little time was actually spent living in or becoming familiar with the community" (Ibid.180), contrary to her professed philosophy. Although declaring an inspired and naïve "calling" to Indian music, Densmore often used coercive methods to gain her highly prized recordings and displayed a need to have complete control over encounters with informants:

> It is not wise to take too many songs from one singer, nor let a man sing too long a time. Singers should be checked by general reputation...men who sing at dances are apt to be too free and easy. The singer must never be allowed to think he is in charge of the work. A strict hold must be kept on him (Ibid.170).

For Densmore, extraneous sounds and impromptu yells were forbidden, and a stick and cardboard box would serve the purpose better than a drum and rattle, if a higher quality recording was the result. Fieldworkers at the turn of the century were under pressure to acquire recordings, since "a collector who failed to return with good material might lose his or her reputation or job" (Ibid.166). Prestige was sometimes a motivating factor as well, evidenced by Frank Cushing's 1880s fieldwork, when his ambition was fulfilled to become a Zuni bowpriest.

The responses of informants to their fieldworker's presence varied from outward resentment to fear of retribution for divulging information or manipulation of the fieldworker to get their needs met in Washington. Wolf Lies Down, of the Crow tribe, took a matter-of-fact approach with fieldworker Robert Lowsie, confronting him about his need to speak "baby talk to the aborigines," and labeled his activities as "familiar and pragmatic as those of a horse trader" (Ibid.164). Walter Fewkes had a frightening night visitation by a Hopi god while working at Walpi, and was believed to be ceremonially induced. Psychic retribution could also affect Indian informants, and was a major concern for many. The Omaha singer Xutha Watonin died shortly after recording for Francis La Flesche, an ethnographer in 1916, and it is believed that his death was a penalty for divulging sacred information (Ibid.165).

By the 1940s, the phonograph itself was under contention with fieldworkers, who claimed it was a hindrance to good relations between collectors and informants. Helen H. Roberts expressed her dislike for using the phonograph in recording Karok and Konomihu music in northern California, because it took away her opportunity for serendipitous discussion with the performers, and hindered her ability to visually concentrate on dances and events around her (Ibid.126). Others found that the performances by individuals were not natural but, rather, strained, as informants sang into the large unusual metal horn of the phonograph. Cylinder recordings continued as the preferred format for recording Indian music until 1936, when they became eclipsed by newer technologies.

Fieldwork was largely put on hold during World War II and, during this period, great changes were about to take place in recording technology. Magnetic tape machines were introduced in 1947 and with them came an ease and portability that allowed enthusiasts to become professionals.

> The introduction of magnetic tape in recording studios, to replace the cumbersome wax masters, put recording technology in everybody's hands. Records could now be made almost everywhere-local radio stations, basements studios, homes-just as long as a pressing company was available to produce discs (Gronow 1983:70).

The long playing disc arrived in 1948, and its capacity to hold longer segments of music would pave the way for the advent of commercial recording companies of American Indian music.

III. Commercial Recording of American Indian Music

> Cities have not so much destroyed groups as refashioned then (Cornell 1988:128).

> The world we know disappears and in changed circumstances we are forced to form new relationships, new responses, new strategies for survival and success, even new conceptions of who we are (Ibid.).

The LP Era, 1950-1969

Within the recording industry at large, the long playing microgroove disc had become the most accepted format by 1948 (Shelemay 1991:282), although disagreements still raged over a standard for playing speed among the traditional 78 RPM, the popular 45 RPM, and the new 33 $^{1/3}$ RPM LP versions. By 1950, the LP was accepted as a norm in the industry as RCA Victor, the last holdout among the major record labels, conceded defeat. Smaller independent companies sprang up eagerly during the 1950s and produced a variety of music styles, but competition with major labels was fierce, so resourceful marketing techniques were needed for these small companies to stay afloat. By 1954, it had become common practice for smaller companies to display their wares at high fidelity shows in major cities and to sell their records at discounted prices (Schick 1979:133-135).

A look at the differences between the 78 RPM and LP formats gives a clearer picture of the changes which were taking place as the first American Indian record companies began production. The 78 RPM discs initially used by these companies could hold four and a half minutes per side, and Eric Brady notes that "this is not enough time to record more than excerpts and segments of ceremonial music and narrative song" (1984:14). With the introduction of the LP disc, which could hold about twenty three minutes of music more traditional versions of songs could be recorded and more songs could be included. Song styles formerly unrelated were combined into anthologies of tribal of Indian music. In the case of one of the first significant record companies, American Indian Soundchiefs, a total of over 300 78 RPM singles each holding two traditional songs, were collated in anthology form onto 97 LP by 1966. At Canyon Records, 82 78 RPMs and 45 RPMs were filtered down to an initial nine LP releases by the same time. In both cases, songs with titles like "Sioux Pipe Dance" or "Laguna Corn Dance" were combined out of context with other songs into homogenous LP with titles like "Sioux" or "Song of the Indian." Although a number of these songs collected from 78s or 45s were released continuously on anthologies throughout later decades, others were simply left behind in an unusable format while many more are unaccounted for.

While there are existing histories of the record industry related to popular music, jazz, and folk music, American Indian music recording has not been examined except as the subject of cataloguing as in Lee (1979) and others. A possible explanation for this deficiency could be the vast difference in the sound of Indian music as compared to Western music.

New recording methods: once informants, now artists

By the early 1940s, individuals with an interest in making traditional Indian music available to the public began recording music for profit. With their names now on record jackets, Indian singers began to attain a sense of fame, even if limited geographically at first. Evaluation of performances could be made by other singers with playback machines, and the beginnings of competitive professional standards defined Indian performers as recording artists rather than informants for anthropological studies. Albeit these differences in methodology existed, curiosity was still focused on music of a bygone era, and the "snapshot for posterity" aesthetic of early anthropologists was carried on by these professionals.

In the 1940s, Manuel Archuleta of San Juan Pueblo, New Mexico, recorded singers at the Indian School in Albuquerque on Tom Tom Records, and published two 78 RPMs entitled "Indian Chants Vol.1 and Vol. 2" (Isaacs 1988:3). Distribution for Archuleta's small company was focused mainly in the Southwest, with Indian and non-Indian record buyers and, as copies of these recordings ran out, the company dissolved (Ibid).

Raymond Boley, a non-Indian music and art lover, whose tastes ranged from opera to world music, was the owner of a film recording studio in Phoenix, Arizona which produced commercials and special events in 1948. After being commissioned to record four songs of Navajo singer Ed Lee Natay for an upcoming play, Boley was taken with the music. He decided to track down Natay in Gallup, New Mexico on year later and Canyon Records' first recording "Natay: Navajo Singer" was produced in three formats: 45, 78, and LP (Boley 1993). Eight LP releases of various traditional tribal music followed in the period from 1950-1969, which were compilations of individually recorded songs from 78 or 45 formats. Boley tried not to record any music which Indians felt was sacred, and his company claimed to go through proper channels, such as tribal offices, before recording. Indian musicians, although pleased to become recording artists, were reticent about the idea of royalty payments, and usually requested cash only. This sentiment is easily understandable, considering past relations with the U.S. government.

Boley, his wife, and a secretary initially made up Canyon Records, and they produced LPs from both recordings made in Indian homelands and from tapes which were mailed to the company by artists. Music was recorded, in both the studio and the field, on reel to reel tape and edited later to take out pauses and "pops." A first pressing from a Los Angeles manufacturer would yield roughly 300 records, which were then peddled to stores on Indian reservations and outlets in nearby cities. Canyon Records established its aesthetic early on, by producing recordings with Isaac's "cross section approach," presenting a musical cross section of a tribal culture (Isaacs 1988:5).

Moses Asch was an entrepreneur with a deeply felt passion for "documenting human aspirations" (Seeger 1991). After two companies failed by naively misjudging the popularity of ethnic recording in the same market as major labels, he finally established the independent Smithsonian Folkways label in 1947, with Harold Courlander. Concurrent with available technology, Asch's first studio efforts in the 1930s were recorded onto wax cylinders and pressed to 78 RPM discs, but by the late 1940s he began using magnetic tape for masters, from which LPs were pressed. Since the Folkways philosophy was to present human aspirations from a global perspective, the American Indian recordings show a cross section approach to tribal music as well.

Recordings collected from the late 1800s and early 1900s by ethnographers previously discussed, were now published on LPs by the Library of Congress label. Recordings were not commercial, in the sense of generating profit for the institution, and the LOC does not, therefore, consider itself a true company. Rather, recordings were a means of disseminating samples of music collected during research projects, and prices barely covered costs (Gray 1993). Titles represented traditional songs from various tribes around the country, and generally show a more in depth approach to production.

In 1966, Indian House Records was established by Tony Isaacs, mainly as an arts and crafts store in Taos, New Mexico. Tony had become interested in American Indian music in the Boy Scouts as a child, and later studied it seriously at U.C.L.A. as an anthropology major. Indian House fulfilled a desire by Isaacs to preserve traditional music which was ebbing as tribes assimilated, and his professed goal was to start an archive of Indian music. He was greatly influenced by the in depth approach of Dr. Linn Pauahty of American Indian Soundchiefs Records. This method of presenting an entire LP of one songtype is closer to what the Indian buying public wants to hear, and more closely parallels the Indian traditional of "lining up" songs for dramatic impact (Isaacs 1988:8).

The aspect of Pauahty's recordings with which Isaacs was not satisfied was the technique of "smothering" the singing and softening the drumming to accommodate studio recorder peak levels. After first traveling to Oklahoma and hearing musicians singing and drumming as loudly as possible, Isaacs decided to portray this in his own recordings. Indian House productions were recorded outdoors with a reel to reel tape recorder, utilizing as large and loud a traditional group as necessary to achieve an authentic performance.

Trends toward intertribalism

Pan-tribal music had been in existence since the 1800s when many ceremonial music and dance forms were outlawed by the U.S. government. The recording industry acted as a catalyst in speeding up the normal diffusion process of intertribal music. The mains reason was an easily exchangeable product in the form of an LP and the resultant wider audiences brought about by this exchange. The two primary forms of intertribal music most popular and recorded frequently by Indian performers during the 1950s and 1960s were powwow and peyote music.

From the 1950s through the 1970s there was an increased interest by Indian people in their individual tribal roots, and also in the pan-tribal Indian pride displayed through powwow music.

It is in the 1950s, 1960s, and 1970s, then, that a supratribal consciousness and constituency were finally made, that Indianization full flowered. It was a protracted process and one of its many parts, reflecting both a changing sociopolitical context made by outsiders and a political agenda-far more constant- made by Indians. Indeed, it has been a continuing product of the encounter between the two (Cornell 1988:139).

Beginning in the 1940s, Reverend Linn Pauahty, a Kiowa Methodist minister from Oklahoma, began recording various Kiowa church hymns throughout Oklahoma on a portable phonodisc machine and manufactured discs with a cutting machine supplied by his church. His newly established record company, American Indian Soundchiefs, produced first 78s, then LPs congruent with industry standards, and distributed primarily to Indian audiences. Pauahty's production aesthetic is what Isaacs refers to as an in depth approach:

> His customers don't want to hear a cross section of a musical culture they already know. If they like round dance songs, they want to hear round dance songs-all round dance songs, maybe 12 or 16 new...songs (Isaacs 1988:6).

Soundchiefs held the largest single catalogue of recordings throughout the 1960s, with roughly 97 titles. The music recorded was specifically Plains Indian, and elucidated contemporary intertribal and intercultural tendencies taking place throughout the 60s, including powwow, peyote ritual, and Indian gospel music.

In 1968, Oscar Humphries started Indian Records in Fay, Oklahoma, with the intent of selling Plains music recordings exclusively to Plains Indian customers. As distribution by other companies spread to the Plains, Indian Records countered by extending sales locations to other areas of the country. Recordings were made on a two track recorder, mostly in the field, in schools, churches, or homes. Productions were pressed by RCA in Indiana or Monarch in Hollywood and released as LPs until roughly 1974 (Humphries 1993).

With a number of independent American Indian record labels established by the 1960s, the style of music recording for all began to shift away from traditional tribal music and toward intertribal styles. Peyote ritual music, powwow and gospel music all contributed to a strength that people from different tribes felt in numbers, and in the sameness of being Indian.

A commercial revival of folk music took place concurrent with the civil rights movement during the 1960s. Some Indian recording artists acquired recording contracts with major record labels, and were able to use this widespread fame as a springboard for social awareness and Indian rights. There were other American Indian musicians who were pioneers in the fields of rock and jazz beginning in the 60s as well.

The record industry at large experienced a drastic change during the 1970s, as phonograph discs were gradually replaced by tapes as the product listeners purchased. More convenient to use, although lacking in the high sound quality of LPs, cassettes could be listened in a car or a home. But the biggest impact of all was that recordings could now be exchanged among listeners, so owners of the original master had essentially lost control over sales of their recordings to the record buyers. Another effect of the introduction of tapes and tape recorders was that Indian artists could now record themselves and submit their master tapes to record companies to help with promotion. Since tapes could be readily exchanged, and the general climate in America was one of cultural interaction and civil rights, other music styles began to influence Indian performers, and we see the beginning of recordings in styles such as gospel, rock, rhythm and blues, jazz and classical, as well as a steady shift toward intertribal genres.

Dealing with an out of control buying market which had access to make copies of recordings at will, the record industry began a shift to the compact disc during the 1980s, and this format has almost completely engulfed the market today. Labels are now, again, in control of sales, even though the piracy of electronic versions of songs from the internet has become prevalent. The main changes in the American Indian music industry since 1980 have mainly been in music styles, with more and more genres added into the repertoire as shifts toward globalization have created a greater melting pot effect. Artists have recorded in styles such as world music, reggae, and new age, while keeping styles that have been historically recorded. There has been a slight shift from a high interest in these styles during the 1990s, back to more traditional intertribal music in the 21st century. Sales of Indian music to a non-Indian audience have dropped dramatically since the 90s, and music is now providing a voice from Native performers for Native performers. Powwow recordings are at an all time high and they are purchased mainly by Native listeners, creating a strengthening of Native culture around the U.S. and Canada. Sadly, there are very few recordings being made today of traditional tribal songs and, as the clock ticks more and more elders who remember these important songs pass.

IV. Native American Music Styles

Traditional tribal music

Traditional music tells the story of the history and legends of each particular tribe or group of Native American people. These are songs for social gatherings, such as the Hopi Butterfly Dance and the Navajo Skip Dance. They can celebrate achievements, rites of passage, special times of the year, or simply be entertainment. Songs can be owned by individuals or families, and are handed down through generations. Tribal customs are continuously kept alive through the regular performance of these songs.

The vast majority of Native American songs are monophonic, with only one melody line, with only a few styles incorporating harmony as well. Singing styles are as rich and varied as the multitude of languages around the United States, Canada, and Mexico. An example is how northern people, such as the Sioux and Blackfoot, generally prefer to sing in a higher pitch range and use a relatively slow drumbeat compared to southern people, like the Kiowa and Pawnee, who prefer a lower pitch range and faster drumbeat. Song structures also differ from region to region. Preferences for song length, form, and number of section repeats vary according to a group's customs, tastes, and artistic symbolism. The sound and rhythm of each particular language has a great influence on the form of each song, as melody and phrases follow the words.

In all styles, solo drumming does not exist. Common to all this music is a voice combined with supporting rhythm, which can consist of drums, shakers, rattles, and jingles. The only melodic instrument on which solo music is played is the flute. The wooden flute originated with the Plains tribes, but is now used throughout North America. Songs are from a traditional tribal context, and include mainly love songs and courting songs.

Intertribal and modern music

In the mid 1800s, tribal customs were being broken down by a dominant U.S. culture. As a result, different styles of intertribal music were created to maintain a sense of common "Indian-ness" and unity among tribes. Pow wows were started in the southern Plains region, and even continue stronger today throughout America and Canada, and around the world. Pow wows create a time and place where common Indian identity is celebrated separate from everyday jobs and activities. They are social events, featuring individual dancers, group singing, social dancing by men, women, and children, gifts, and prizes.

Pow wows today have taken on a semi professional character, as singing groups, called "drums," make live recordings and compete for cash prizes. Singers have traditionally been men, but recently more women singers are entering the field. Singers gather around a large pow wow drum, play it together, and follow the lead singer in a call and response style of singing. The sound of the large double headed drum thunders as a central heartbeat throughout a song, with some skips and changes in timbre, volume, but always the same tempo for the dancers.

Pow wow songs developed over time from the older grass dance songs of the Kiowa, Pawnee, and Ponca tribes. The southern songs tend to use a medium drum tempo, and a relaxed and rich tenor singing style. As the pow wow celebration spread to northern Plains tribes, new music styles evolved from the Sioux, Cree, and Blackfoot people. The northern style has a slow drum tempo and is sung in a very high pitched tense nasal style.

Native American Church music, or peyote ritual music, began to spread at the same time as pow wow music, as a way of maintaining Indian identity. Peyote ritual songs are performed during night long ceremonies used for healing and spiritual regeneration. A peyote song is sung in a chant style and accompanied by the rapid and constant soft beating of a water drum. This drum is made from a ceramic bowl or metal bowl, filled with water and covered with a tight animal skin head. The water drum produces a unique soft and penetrating sound that can induce transformation in the listener. A special rattle, made of a gourd and decorated with symbolic feathers, is shaken throughout a song, in tempo with the drum.

Chicken Scratch music, or Waila, is a modern style which has come to be accepted as a traditional form of music among the O'Odham people of southern Arizona. Chicken Scratch is a unique blending of the traditional song styles of the O'Odham, with polka songs and instruments brought by German railroad workers living in Arizona in the 1800s, along with Mexican norteño music, as these three groups of people commonly celebrated together. Nowadays, Scratch groups consist of drums, electric bass, saxophone, electric guitar, and accordion, and bands play at all night dance parties under the desert stars.

18

References Cited

Brady, Erika
        1985   "The Box that Flourishes: The Cylinder Phonograph in Folklore
                Fieldwork, 1890-1937." Ph.D. dissertation, Indiana University.

        1984   *The Federal Cylinder Project.* Vol. 1, *Introduction and Inventory.*
                Washington, D.C.: American Folklife Center, Library of
                Congress.

Brown, Dee
        1970   *Bury My Heart at Wounded Knee.* New York: Henry Holt and
                Company.

Boley, Raymond, founder and former owner of Canyon Records
        1993   Interview by author. February 18. Phoenix, Arizona.

Cornell, Stephen
        1988   *The Return of the Native: American Indian Political Resurgence.*
                New York: Oxford University Press.

Debo, Angie
        1972   *A History of the Indians of the United States.* Norman: University
                of Oklahoma Press.

Deloria, Vine and Clifford M. Lytle
        1984   *The Nations Within: The Past and Future of American Indian
                Sovereignty.* New York: Pantheon Books.

Densmore, Frances
        1936   *Cheyenne and Arapaho Music.* Los Angeles: Southwest
                Museum.

        1926   *The American Indians and Their Music.* New York: The Woman's
                Press.

Fletcher, Alice C.
        1893   "A Study of Omaha Indian Music" in *Archeological and
                Ethnological Papers of the Peabody Museum.* Vol. 1. No. 5.
                Harvard University.

Gray, Judith
        1993   Personal letter accompanying the Library of Congress catalogue
                of recordings.

Gronow, Pekka
    1983   "The Record Industry: The Growth of a Mass Medium" in <u>Popular Music</u> 3:53-76.
Hinton, Leanne
    1985   "Musical Diffusion and Linguistic Diffusion" in *Explorations in Ethnomusicology: Essays in Honor of David P. McAllester.* Charlotte J. Frisbie, ed. Detroit Monographs in Musicology, Number 9. Detroit: Information Coordinators.

Hofman, Charles, ed.
    1968   *Frances Densmore and American Indian Music.* (Contributions from the Museum of the American Indian, Heye Foundation. Volume XXIII. New York: Museum of the American Indian.

Isaacs, Tony, founder and owner of Indian House Records
    1993   Interview by author. March 15. Arroyo Seco, New Mexico.

    1988   "Collecting Native American Music," paper presented at the Thirty-first Annual Meeting of the College Music Society. Santa Fe, New Mexico. October 14.

Lame Deer, John and Richard Erdoes
    1972   *Lame Deer, Seeker of Visions.* New York: Simon and Schuster, Inc.

Lee, Dorothy Sara
    1979   *Native North American Music and Oral Data: A Catalogue of Sound Recordings, 1893-1976.* Bloomington: Indiana University Press.

Neihardt, John C.
    1932   *Black Elk Speaks.* New York: Washington Square Press.

Scabby Robe, Kenny, lead singer, Black Lodge Singers, educator.
    1993   Interview by author. January 31. Scottsdale, Arizona.

Schicke, C.A.
    1973   *Revolution in Sound: A Biography of the Recording Industry.* Boston: Little, Brown and Company.

Seeger, Anthony, Head Curator, Smithsonian/Folkways Records.
    1993   Interview by author. February 16. Tempe, Arizona.

    1986   "The Role of Sound Archives in Ethnomusicology Today" in <u>Ethnomusicology</u> 30/2:261-276.

20

Shelemay, Kay Kaufman

    1991   "Recording Technology, the Record Industry, and Ethnomusicological Scholarship" in *Comparative Musicology and Anthropology of Music*. Bruno Nettl and Phillip V. Bohlman, eds. Chicago: The University of Chicago Press.

    1990   *The Garland Library Readings in Ethnomusicology*. Volume 6. New York: Garland Publishing.

Discography of Native American Music
Currently Available

Pow Wow Music

24

Canadian Pow Wow Groups

A-1 Club Singers
Vol.2, Pow-Wow Songs
CANYON RECORDS CR-9007, Recorded: Studio, Format: Cassette

Assiniboine Jr.
Assiniboine Jr. Singers
SUNSHINE RECORDS SSCT 4117, Recorded: Studio, Format: Cassette

Vol.3 Pow-Wow Songs
CANYON RECORDS CR-16229, Recorded: Studio, Format: Cassette

Vol.4, live at O'odham Tash
CANYON RECORDS CR-16230, Recorded: Live, Format: Cassette

Vol.5, Pow Wow Songs
CANYON RECORDS CR-16231, Recorded: Studio, Format: Cassette

Bad Medicine
Blast From the Past
SWEET GRASS RECORDS SGBM082501, Recorded: Studio, Format: CD

Battle River
Couple for the Road
Arbor Records AR11052 (CD) AR11054 (Cassette), Recorded: Studio

Bear Creek
LIVE
Arbor Records AR11512 (CD), AR11514 (Cassette), Recorded: Live

The Show Must Go On
Arbor Records AR 11992 (CD), AR11994 (Cassette, Recorded: Studio

Big Bear
Spirit Dancer
SWEET GRASS RECORDS SGBB32100, Recorded: Studio, Format: CD, Cassette

Black Hills
16th Annual Pow Wow
Arbor Records AR11962, Recorded: Live: Format: CD

Blackfoot Singers
Vol.1, Pow-Wow Songs
CANYON RECORDS CR-6132, Recorded: Studio, Format: Cassette

Blackfoot A-1 Club Singers
> *Volume 1*
> INDIAN HOUSE RECORDS 4001
> Contents: A-1 Club theme songs, 4 war dance songs, 2 chicken dance songs
> Singers: Andy Axe, Dennis Black Rider, Nick Breaker, Ralph Crow Chief,
> Raymond Crow Chief, Phillip Little Chief, Gerald Sitting Eagle, Marcel Weasel
> Head
> Recorded: at Gleichen, Alberta, July 26, 1972
> Tribe: Blackfoot
> Format: Cassette, LP

> *Volume 2*
> INDIAN HOUSE RECORDS 4002
> Contents: 2 war dance songs, 1 competition song, 3 chicken dance songs, 6 owl
> dance songs
> Singers: Andy Axe, Dennis Black Rider, Nick Breaker, Ralph Crow Chief,
> Raymond Crow Chief, Phillip Little Chief, Gerald Sitting Eagle, Marcel Weasel
> Head
> Recorded: at Gleichen, Alberta, July 26, 1972--Continued from INDIAN HOUSE
> RECORDS 4001
> Tribe: Blackfoot
> Format: Cassette, LP

Blackfoot Crossing
> *Blackfoot Crossing*
> INDIAN HOUSE RECORDS 4003
> Contents: 11 grass dance songs, 2 shake dance songs, 2 stomp songs
> Singers: Fred Breaker, Eldon Weasel Child, Radford Blackrider, Rod Scout,
> Herman Yellow Old Woman, Dennis Blackrider, Julius Delaney, Frederick
> Johnson, Irvin Johnson
> Recorded: at Gleichen, Alberta, August 12, 1989
> Tribe: Blackfoot
> Format: Cassette

Blackstone Singers
> *Vol.1, Contest Songs Live!*
> CANYON RECORDS CR-16217, Recorded: Live, Format: Cassette

> *Vol.2, Live at Fort Duchesne*
> CANYON RECORDS CR-16218, Recorded: Live, Format: Cassette

> *Vol.3, Pow-Wow Songs*
> CANYON RECORDS CR-16219, Recorded: Studio, Format: Cassette

> *Vol.4, Pow-Wow Recorded Live!*
> CANYON RECORDS CR-16256, Recorded: Live, Format: Cassette

> *Vol.5, Pow-Wow Recorded Live!*
> CANYON RECORDS CR-16257, Recorded: Live, Format: Cassette

> *Vol.6, Pow Wow Songs*
> CANYON RECORDS CR-16258, Recorded: Studio, Format: Cassette

Vol. 7, Around the Horn
CANYON RECORDS CR-6352, Recorded: Studio, Format: Cassette

Vol. 8, Pictures of You
CANYON RECORDS CR-6353, Recorded: Studio, Format: Cassette

The Boyz
Life and Times of TBZ
Arbor Records AR11292 (CD) AR11294 (Cassette), Recorded: Studio

Brown Eagle
Brown Eagle
SUNSHINE RECORDS SSCT 4147, Recorded: Studio, Format: Cassette

Brown Eagle Vol. II
SUNSHINE RECORDS SSCT 4175, Recorded: Studio, Format: Cassette

Brown Eagle Vol. III
SUNSHINE RECORDS SSCT 4197, Recorded: Studio, Format: Cassette

Buffalo Lake Singers
Buffalo Lake Singers
SUNSHINE RECORDS SSCT 4184, Recorded: Studio, Format: Cassette

Schemitzun 2000
SWEET GRASS RECORDS SGBL091700, Recorded: Studio, Format: CD, Cassette

Burntside Lake
Str8 Up
Arbor Records AR11212 (CD) AR11214 (Cassette), Recorded: Studio

Cache Lake
Keeping the Tradition
SWEET GRASS RECORDS SGS62696, Recorded: Studio, Format: Cassette

Calf Robe Singers
Family Pow Wow
SOAR 135, Recorded: Studio, Format: CD, Cassette

Vol.1, The Next Generation
CANYON RECORDS CR-16226, Recorded: Studio, Format: Cassette

Vol.2, Pow-Wow Songs
CANYON RECORDS CR-16227, Recorded: Studio, Format: Cassette

Cathedral Lakes Singers
American Pow Wow
SOAR 142, Recorded: Studio, Format: CD, Cassette

Live at Window Rock
CANYON RECORDS CR-6296, Recorded: Live, Format: Cassette

Pow Wow Songs Vol. 1
SOAR 116, Recorded: Studio, Format: CD, Cassette

Pow Wow Songs Vol. 2
SOAR 122, Recorded: Studio, Format: CD, Cassette

Pow Wow Songs Vol. 3
SOAR 134, Recorded: Studio, Format: CD, Cassette

Cedar Dale
Southern Style
Arbor Records AR11112 (CD) AR11114 (Cassette), Recorded: Studio

Cedar Tree
Schemitzun '96
SWEET GRASS RECORDS SGC91896, Recorded: Studio, Format: CD

Chief Jimmy Bruneau School Drummers
Drum Dance Music of the Dogrib
CANYON RECORDS CR-16260, Recorded: Studio, Format: Cassette

Chi-Geezis Singers
Chi-Geezis Singers
SUNSHINE RECORDS SSCT 4277, Recorded: Studio, Format: Cassette

Songs of the Ojibway/Odawa
SUNSHINE RECORDS SSCT 4276, Recorded: Studio, Format: Cassette

Chi_Nodin Singers
Chi_Nodin Singers
SUNSHINE RECORDS SSCT 4293, Recorded: Studio, Format: Cassette

Live at Batchewana
SWEET GRASS RECORDS SGC9696, Recorded: Studio, Format: Cassette

Chiniki Lake Singers
Chiniki Lake Singers
SUNSHINE RECORDS SSCT 4178, Recorded: Studio, Format: Cassette

Vol.1, Pow-Wow Songs
CANYON RECORDS CR-9003, Recorded: Studio, Format: Cassette

Circle Strong Singers
Circle Strong Singers
SUNSHINE RECORDS SSCT 4249, Recorded: Studio, Format: Cassette

Cree Spirit
Cree Spirit
SUNSHINE RECORDS SSCT 4142, Recorded: Studio, Format: Cassette

Cree Spirit Vol. II
SUNSHINE RECORDS SSCT 4159, Recorded: Studio, Format: Cassette

Cree Spirit Vol. III
SUNSHINE RECORDS SSCT 4208, Recorded: Studio, Format: Cassette

Cree Spirit Vol. IV
SUNSHINE RECORDS SSCT 4245, Recorded: Studio, Format: Cassette

Cree White Tail
Live at Toronto Sky Dome
SWEET GRASS RECORDS SGC112997, Recorded: Studio, Format: CD, Cassette

Crowfoot Drummers
Blackfoot Pow-Wow Songs
CANYON RECORDS CR-9009, Recorded: Studio, Format: Cassette

Crooked Lake Agency
Good Ol' Days
SWEET GRASS RECORDS SGCL4997, Recorded: Studio, Format: CD, Cassette

Crowe Singers
Crowe Singers
Arbor Records AR11362 (CD) AR11364 (Cassette), Recorded: Studio

Dakota Travels
Live@ Prairie Island
Arbor Records AR11622 (CD) AR11624 (Cassette), Recorded: Live

Delia, the Waskewitch Boys
Round Dance
SWEET GRASS RECORDS SGD051501, Recorded: Studio, Format: CD

Drumming Hill
Volume 1
SWEET GRASS RECORDS SGDH72197, Recorded: Studio, Format: CD, Cassette

Eagle Claw
Eagle Claw
SUNSHINE RECORDS SSCT 4207, Recorded: Studio, Format: Cassette

Eagle Claw and Kirby Littletent
Eagle Claw & Kirby Littletent
SUNSHINE RECORDS SSCT 4299, Recorded: Studio, Format: Cassette

Eagle Creek
Eagle Creek
SUNSHINE RECORDS SSCT 4213, Recorded: Studio, Format: Cassette

Eagle Hill
Eagle Hill
SUNSHINE RECORDS SSCT 4144, Recorded: Studio, Format: Cassette

Eagle Tail

Eagle Tail
SUNSHINE RECORDS SSCT 4140, Recorded: Studio, Format: Cassette

Eagle Tail Vol II
SUNSHINE RECORDS SSCT 4177, Recorded: Studio, Format: Cassette

Singing for the People
SWEET GRASS RECORDS SGET41699, Recorded: Studio, Format: CD, Cassette

Eagle Society

Blackfoot Grass Dance Songs - Siksika Nation
INDIAN HOUSE RECORDS 4011
Contents: 5 grass dance songs, 4 war dance songs, 2 fancy dance songs, Robert Sun Walk Family song
Singers: Robert Sun Walk, Henry Sun Walk, Donald Scalplock, Irvine Scalplock, Clarence Wolfleg, Ed Calf Robe Jr., Trent Sun Walk, Wesley Sun Walk, Garry Sun Walk
Recorded: at Cluny, Alberta, September 21, 1989
Tribe: Blackfoot
Format: Cassette

Eagle Tail

Jammin' on the Rez
Arbor Records AR11642 (CD) AR11644 (Cassette), Recorded: Studio

Earlwin B. Bullhead

Father to Son
Arbor Records AR11692 (CD) AR11694 (Cassette), Recorded: Studio

Eastern Eagle Singers

Sacred Flight
Arbor Records AR11602 (CD) AR11604 (Cassette), Recorded: Studio

Eden Valley Singers

Stoney Pow-Wow Songs
CANYON RECORDS CR-6136, Recorded: Studio, Format: Cassette

Edmund Bull

I've Been Everywhere
SWEET GRASS RECORDS SGEBCD120294, Recorded: Studio, Format: CD

Ermineskin Powwow

Live at Bear Park
SWEET GRASS RECORDS SGE80199, Recorded: Studio, Format: CD, Cassette

Eyabay

Ain't Nuthin But A Thang
SUNSHINE RECORDS, Recorded: Studio, Format: CD SSCD4397, Tape SSCT4397

Live 2000
Arbor Records AR11182 (CD) AR11184 (Cassette), Recorded: Live

Miracle
Arbor Records AR11612 (CD) AR11614 (Cassette), Recorded: Studio

No Limit
Arbor Records AR11012 (CD) AR11014 (Cassette), Recorded: Studio

Pow-Wow Songs Recorded Live!
CANYON RECORDS CR-16250, Recorded: Live, Format: Cassette

First Nation Singers
First Nation Singers
SUNSHINE RECORDS SSCT 4183, Recorded: Studio, Format: Cassette

Fly-in Eagle
Assorted Artists
SUNSHINE RECORDS SSCT 4168, Recorded: Studio, Format: Cassette

Fly In Eagle Singers
SUNSHINE RECORDS SSCT 4164, Recorded: Studio, Format: Cassette

Vol.1, Pow Wow Songs
CANYON RECORDS CR-16232, Recorded: Studio, Format: Cassette

Vol.2, The Straighter the Better
CANYON RECORDS CR-16233, Recorded: Studio, Format: Cassette

Vol.3, The 2nd Wave: Straight Songs
CANYON RECORDS CR-6234, Recorded: Studio, Format: Cassette

Vol.4, Red and Blue - Pow-Wow Songs
CANYON RECORDS CR-6236, Recorded: Studio, Format: Cassette

Four Little Feathers
Four Little Feathers
SUNSHINE RECORDS SSCT 4141, Recorded: Studio, Format: Cassette

Four Wings Singers
Four Wings Singers
SUNSHINE RECORDS SSCT 4267, Recorded: Studio, Format: Cassette

Free Spirit
Free Spirit
SUNSHINE RECORDS SSCT 4093, Recorded: Studio, Format: Cassette

Grassy Narrows Singers
Grassy Narrows Singers
SUNSHINE RECORDS SSCT 4296, Recorded: Studio, Format: Cassette

Grey Buffalo Singers
Grey Buffalo Singers
SUNSHINE RECORDS SSCT 4126, Recorded: Studio, Format: Cassette

Grey Buffalo Singers Vol. II
SUNSHINE RECORDS SSCT 4238, Recorded: Studio, Format: Cassette

Grey Eagle
Blue Moon of Kehewin
SWEET GRASS RECORDS SGGE12099, Recorded: Studio, Format: CD, Cassette

Hanisha Traditional Singers
Hanisha Traditonal Singers
SUNSHINE RECORDS SSCT 4273, Recorded: Studio, Format: Cassette

Hanisha Traditional Singers Vol. II
SUNSHINE RECORDS SSCT 2492-4, Recorded: Studio, Format: Cassette

Hawk River
Nikoodi Rhythm
SUNSHINE RECORDS SSCT 4157, Recorded: Studio, Format: Cassette

Hi Bull Singers
Hi Bull Singers
SUNSHINE RECORDS SSCT 4162, Recorded: Studio, Format: Cassette

High Noon
High Noon '97
SWEET GRASS RECORDS SGHN20997, Recorded: Studio, Format: CD, Cassette

Iron Wood
Schemitzun '97
SWEET GRASS RECORDS SGIW90697, Recorded: Studio, Format: CD

Kai-Spai Singers
Songs from the Blood Reserve
CANYON RECORDS CR-6133, Recorded: Studio, Format: Cassette

Kau-Ta-Noh Jrs.
Kau-Ta-Noh Jrs.
SUNSHINE RECORDS, Recorded: Studio, Format: CD SSCD4446, Tape SSCT4446

Kicking Woman
A Tribute to Merlin Kicking Woman Jr
SWEET GRASS RECORDS SGKW62597, Recorded: Studio, Format: Cassette

Kingbird Singers
Chippewa Grass Dance Songs
CANYON RECORDS CR-6106, Recorded: Studio, Format: Cassette

Kingbird Singers at White Earth 1979
CANYON RECORDS CR-6170, Recorded: Live, Format: Cassette

Lake of the Woods
Songs of Thunder
Arbor Records AR 11372 (CD) AR11374 (Cassette), Recorded: Studio

Little Axe
In Honor of Art Scaplock
SWEET GRASS RECORDS SGLA12598, Recorded: Studio, Format: CD, Cassette

Live At Beardy's
SWEET GRASS RECORDS SGLA81598, Recorded: Studio, Format: CD, Cassette

Little Boy Singers
Vol.1, Pow-Wow Songs
CANYON RECORDS CR-6206, Recorded: Studio, Format: Cassette

Vol.2, Intertribal Pow-Wow Songs
CANYON RECORDS CR-6207, Recorded: Studio, Format: Cassette

Vol.3, Round Dance Songs
CANYON RECORDS CR-6220, Recorded: Studio, Format: Cassette

Vol.4, Intertribal Pow-Wow Songs
CANYON RECORDS CR-16221, Recorded: Studio, Format: Cassette

Vol.5, Round Dance Songs

Little Island Cree
For Old Times' Sake
SWEET GRASS RECORDS SGLI11399, Recorded: Studio, Format: CD, Cassette

Indian Country
SWEET GRASS RECORDS SGLI12800, Recorded: Studio, Format: CD, Cassette

Little Island Cree
SUNSHINE RECORDS SSCT 4181, Recorded: Studio, Format: Cassette

Little Island Cree, Friends
SWEET GRASS RECORDS SGLIC103099, Recorded: Studio, Format: CD, Cassette

Live at Beardy's
SWEET GRASS RECORDS SGLIC81698, Recorded: Live, Format: CD, Cassette

Round Dance
SWEET GRASS RECORDS SGLI9696, Recorded: Studio, Format: Cassette

Little Otter
Little Otter
SUNSHINE RECORDS SSCT 4171, Recorded: Studio, Format: Cassette
CANYON RECORDS CR-16222, Recorded: Studio, Format: Cassette

The Return
Arbor Records AR11812 (CD) AR11814 (Cassette), Recorded: Liv

Little Pine Singers
Cree Pow-Wow Songs
CANYON RECORDS CR-6169, Recorded: Studio, Format: Cassette

Little Spirit Singers
Little Spirit Singers
SUNSHINE RECORDS SSCT 4272, Recorded: Studio, Format: Cassette

Logan Alexis Singers
I Love to Round Dance
SWEET GRASS RECORDS SGLA40197, Recorded: Studio, Format: Cassette

Logan Alexis Singers Vol. II
SUNSHINE RECORDS SSCT 4288, Recorded: Studio, Format: Cassette

Logan Alexis Singers Round Dance
SUNSHINE RECORDS SSCT 4130, Recorded: Studio, Format: Cassette

Lone Eagle Creek Singers
Lone Eagle Creek Singers
SUNSHINE RECORDS SSCT 4198, Recorded: Studio, Format: Cassette

Mandaree
For the People
Arbor Records AR11322 (CD) AR11324 (Cassette), Recorded: Studio

McGilvery, Green
Shining Elbow
SWEET GRASS RECORDS SGMG61798, Recorded: Studio, Format: CD, Cassette

Mervin Dreaver
Gone But Not Forgotten
SWEET GRASS RECORDS SGMD12898, Recorded: Studio, Format: CD, Cassette

Moccasin Flat
Tribal Heat
SWEET GRASS RECORDS SGMF12398, Recorded: Studio, Format: CD, Cassette

Mosquito

For the Young at Heart
SWEET GRASS RECORDS SGM11079, Recorded: Studio, Format: Cassette

Keep Me in Your Heart
SWEET GRASS RECORDS SGM101995, Recorded: Studio, Format: Cassette

You Belong to Me
SWEET GRASS RECORDS SGM102897, Recorded: Studio, Format: CD, Cassette

Mountain Soul

Soul Lives On
SWEET GRASS RECORDS SGMS61500, Recorded: Studio, Format: CD, Cassette

Mystic River Singers

Mystic River Singers
SUNSHINE RECORDS SSCT 4251, Recorded: Studio, Format: Cassette

Schemitzun '96
SWEET GRASS RECORDS SGMR92096, Recorded: Studio, Format: CD

Nakda Lodge

Dark Realm
SUNSHINE RECORDS, Recorded: Studio, Format: CD SSCD4425, Tape SSCT4425

Na Gamodaa

Let's Sing
SWEET GRASS RECORDS SGNW61297, Recorded: Studio, Format: CD, Cassette

North Buffalo Cree Jrs.

North Buffalo Cree Jrs.
SUNSHINE RECORDS SSCT 4228, Recorded: Studio, Format: Cassette

Northern Cree Singers

Double Platinum
CANYON RECORDS CR-6347, Recorded: Studio, Format: Cassette

Northern Cree and Friends
CANYON RECORDS CR-6350, Recorded: Studio, Format: Cassette

Still Rezin'
CANYON RECORDS CR-6358, Recorded: Studio, Format: Cassette

Vol.1, Pow-Wow Songs
CANYON RECORDS CR-16210, Recorded: Studio, Format: Cassette

Vol.2, Pow-Wow Songs
CANYON RECORDS CR-16211, Recorded: Studio, Format: Cassette

Vol.3, Live at Fort Duchesne
CANYON RECORDS CR-16212, Recorded: Live, Format: Cassette

Vol.4, "No word songs please"
CANYON RECORDS CR-16240, Recorded: Studio, Format: Cassette

Vol.5, Pow-Wow Songs
CANYON RECORDS CR-16241, Recorded: Studio, Format: Cassette

Vol.6, Pow-Wow Recorded Live!
CANYON RECORDS CR-16242, Recorded: Live, Format: Cassette

Vol.7, Come & Dance
CANYON RECORDS CR-6246, Recorded: Studio, Format: Cassette

Vol.9, Dance Hard!
CANYON RECORDS CR-6247, Recorded: Studio, Format: Cassette

Vol.10, Honor the Eagle Feather
CANYON RECORDS CR-6269, Recorded: Studio, Format: Cassette

Vol.11, It's Time to Round Dance
CANYON RECORDS CR-6292, Recorded: Studio, Format: Cassette

Vol.12, In Our Drum We Trust
CANYON RECORDS CR-6291, Recorded: Studio, Format: Cassette

Vol.13, Here to Stay
CANYON RECORDS CR-6321, Recorded: Studio, Format: Cassette

Vol.14, Showtime
CANYON RECORDS CR-6322, Recorded: Studio, Format: Cassette

Vol.15, Rockin' the Rez
CANYON RECORDS CR-6327, Recorded: Studio, Format: Cassette

Vol.16, Second Song... Dancer's Choice!
CANYON RECORDS CR-6331, Recorded: Studio, Format: Cassette

Vol. 17, Round Dance Jam
CANYON RECORDS CR-6346, Recorded: Studio, Format: Cassette

Northern Wind
21st Century
Arbor Records AR11122 (CD) AR11124 (Cassette, Recorded: Studio

Campfire
Arbor Records AR11572 (CD) AR11574 (Cassette), Recorded: Studio

Dance with Us
Arbor Records AR11392 (CD) AR11394 (Cassette), Recorded: Studio

Jingle Dress Songs
Arbor Records AR 11282 (CD) AR11284 (Cassette), Recorded: Studio

Northern Wind
SUNSHINE RECORDS SSCT 4108, Recorded: Studio, Format: Cassette

Northern Wind Vol. II
SUNSHINE RECORDS SSCT 4128, Recorded: Studio, Format: Cassette

Northern Wind Vol. III
SUNSHINE RECORDS SSCT 4154, Recorded: Studio, Format: Cassette

Northern Wind Vol. IV
SUNSHINE RECORDS SSCT 4170, Recorded: Studio, Format: Cassette

Northern Wind Vol. V
SUNSHINE RECORDS SSCT 4195, Recorded: Studio, Format: Cassette

Northern Wind Vol. VI: Jingle Dress Songs
SUNSHINE RECORDS SSCT 4205, Recorded: Studio, Format: Cassette

Northern Wind Vol. VII
SUNSHINE RECORDS SSCT 4239, Recorded: Studio, Format: Cassette

Northern Wind Vol. VIII
SUNSHINE RECORDS SSCT 4271, Recorded: Studio, Format: Cassette

Schemitzun '97
SWEET GRASS RECORDS SGNW90587, Recorded: Studio, Format: CD,
Cassette

Oak Dale
Live at CTK
SWEET GRASS RECORDS SGO72796, Recorded: Studio, Format: Cassette

Old Agency Singers of the Blood Reserve
Volume 1
INDIAN HOUSE RECORDS 4051
Contents: 5 grass dance songs, 3 chicken dance songs
Singers: Jim Chief Calf, John Chief Calf, Dominic Cross Child, Jarvie Day Chief,
Dean Plume, Dan Weasel Moccasin Sr., Daniel Weasel Moccasin Jr., Stewart
Weasel Moccasin
Recorded: at Stand Off, Alberta, July 27, 1972
Tribe: Blood
Format: Cassette

Volume 2
INDIAN HOUSE RECORDS 4052
Contents: 2 grass dance songs, 2 chicken dance songs, 4 owl dance songs
Singers: Jim Chief Calf, John Chief Calf, Dominic Cross Child, Dick Day Chief, Jarvie Day Chief, Dean Plume, Dan Weasel Moccasin Sr., Daniel Weasel Moccasin Jr., Stewart Weasel Moccasin
Recorded: at Stand Off, Alberta, July 27, 1972--Continued from INDIAN HOUSE RECORDS 4051
Tribe: Blood
Format: Cassette, LP

Omaha White Tail
For the Mothers
SWEET GRASS RECORDS SGW72998, Recorded: Studio, Format: CD

Live at CTK
SWEET GRASS RECORDS SGWT72696, Recorded: Studio, Format: Cassette

Live at Red Earth
SWEET GRASS RECORDS SGWT61397, Recorded: Studio, Format: CD, Cassette

Painted Horse
Good Ole Days
SWEET GRASS RECORDS SGPH4297, Recorded: Studio, Format: CD, Cassette

Just Horsin' Around
SWEET GRASS RECORDS SGPH4397, Recorded: Studio, Format: CD, Cassette

Live at Napi
SWEET GRASS RECORDS SGPH12498, Recorded: Studio, Format: CD, Cassette

Painted Horse
SWEET GRASS RECORDS SGPH010696, Recorded: Studio, Format: CD

Pigeon Lake Singers
Pigeon Lake Singers
SUNSHINE RECORDS SSCT 4148, Recorded: Studio, Format: Cassette

Vol.1, Cree Tribal Songs
CANYON RECORDS CR-6163, Recorded: Studio, Format: Cassette

Vol.2, Pow-Wow Songs
CANYON RECORDS CR-9001, Recorded: Studio, Format: Cassette

Vol.3, Pow-Wow Songs
CANYON RECORDS CR-16264, Recorded: Studio, Format: Cassette

Pipestone
Arbor Records AR11632 (CD) AR11634 (Cassette), Recorded: Studio

Plains Indian Singers
Pow-Wow Songs
CANYON RECORDS CR-16255, Recorded: Studio, Format: Cassette

Plains Ojibway Singers
Plains Ojibway Singers
SUNSHINE RECORDS SSCT 4120, Recorded: Studio, Format: Cassette

Poor Boys
Oklahoma'
Arbor Records AR11822 (CD) AR11824 (Cassette), Recorded: Studio

Red Bull Singers
The Best of Red Bull
SWEET GRASS RECORDS SGRB101599, Recorded: Studio, Format: CD, Cassette

Dancing Around the World
SWEET GRASS RECORDS SGRB051595, Recorded: Studio, Format: CD, Cassette

Gather the People
CANYON RECORDS CR-6277, Recorded: Studio, Format: Cassette

Have a Good Time
CANYON RECORDS CR-16265, Recorded: Studio, Format: Cassette

Having Fun Dancing
SWEET GRASS RECORDS SGRB101693, Recorded: Studio, Format: Cassette

Millennium
SWEET GRASS RECORDS SGRB11200, Recorded: Studio, Format: CD, Cassette

Mother Earth
SWEET GRASS RECORDS SGRB012296, Recorded: Studio, Format: CD, Cassette

Red Bull, Volume 2
SUNSHINE RECORDS, Recorded: Studio, Format: CD SSCD4377, Tape SSCT4377

World Handdrum Champions
SWEET GRASS RECORDS SGRB90498, Recorded: Studio, Format: CD, Cassette

Red Dog
> *Plain, Simple*
> SWEET GRASS RECORDS SGRD052001, Recorded: Studio, Format: CD,
> Cassette

Red Hawk Singers
> *Red Hawk Singers*
> SUNSHINE RECORDS SSCT 4266, Recorded: Studio, Format: Cassette
>
> *Red Hawk Singers Vol. II*
> SWEET GRASS RECORDS (No Number), Recorded: Studio, Format: Cassette

Red Scaffold
> *Red Scaffold*
> SUNSHINE RECORDS SSCT 4212, Recorded: Studio, Format: Cassette

Red Shadow Singers
> *Red Shadow Singers*
> SUNSHINE RECORDS SSCT 4165, Recorded: Studio, Format: Cassette

Red Sons Singers
> *Red Sons Singers*
> SWEET GRASS RECORDS (No Number), Recorded: Studio, Format: Cassette

Red House
> **Between Two Worlds**
> Arbor Records AR11952, Recorded: Studio, Format: CD
>
> **Round Dancin' Back to Cali...**
> Arbor Records AR121502 (CD) AR11504 (Cassette), Recorded: Studio

Red Tail
> *Volume 1*
> Arbor Records AR11264, Recorded: Studio, Format: Cassette
>
> *Volume 2*
> Arbor Records AR11432 (CD) AR11434 (Cassette), Recorded: Studio

Red Wind
> *Red Wind*
> SUNSHINE RECORDS SSCT 4297, Recorded: Studio, Format: Cassette

River Cree
> *Livin' in the Rez*
> Arbor Records AR11542 (CD) AR11544 (Cassette), Recorded: Studio

Sarcee Broken Knife
> *Vol.2, Pow-Wow Songs*
> CANYON RECORDS CR-9011, Recorded: Studio, Format: Cassette

S.E.C.C Earth Band
2nd Annual Cherokee Festival
SUNSHINE RECORDS SSCT 4268, Recorded: Studio, Format: Cassette

Saulteaux First Nation Singers
Round Dance
SWEET GRASS RECORDS SGS102698, Recorded: Studio, Format: CD,
Cassette

Schemitzun World Championship of Song, Dance
Hand Drum Songs
SWEET GRASS RECORDS SGRD091500, Recorded: Live, Format: CD,
Cassette

Seekaskootch
Guardian of the People
SWEET GRASS RECORDS SGS71197, Recorded: Studio, Format: CD,
Cassette

Seekaskootch
SUNSHINE RECORDS SSCT 4182, Recorded: Studio, Format: Cassette

Shake the Feathers Peguis Pow Wow '93
SUNSHINE RECORDS SSCT 4204, Recorded: Live, Format: Cassette

Sinte Ska: Sounds of the Pow Wow
SUNSHINE RECORDS SSCT 4185, Recorded: Studio, Format: Cassette

Shadow Prey
Shadow Prey
SWEET GRASS RECORDS SGSH1120595, Recorded: Studio, Format:
Cassette

Sizzortail
Enuff Said
Arbor Records AR11142 (CD) AR 11144 (Cassette), Recorded: Studio

Siksika Ramblers
Just for Old Times Sakes
CANYON RECORDS CR-6287, Recorded: Studio, Format: Cassette

Straight from the Rez
CANYON RECORDS CR-6323, Recorded: Studio, Format: Cassette

Owl Dance of the Siksika Nation
CANYON RECORDS CR-6332, Recorded: Studio, Format: Cassette

Sioux Assiniboine
Kahomini Songs
SUNSHINE RECORDS SSCT 4115, Recorded: Studio, Format: Cassette

Sioux Assiniboine
SUNSHINE RECORDS SSCT 4187, Recorded: Studio, Format: Cassette

Sioux Assniboine Vol. II
SUNSHINE RECORDS SSCT 4136, Recorded: Studio, Format: Cassette

Sioux Assiniboine Vol. III
SUNSHINE RECORDS SSCT 4152, Recorded: Studio, Format: Cassette

Smokey Town Singers
Smokey Town Singers
SUNSHINE RECORDS SSCT 4221, Recorded: Studio, Format: Cassette

Smokey Valley
West Coast Footslide
Arbor Records AR11892 (CD) AR11894 (Cassette), Recorded: Studio

Southern Boys
Brothers for Life
Arbor Records AR11552 (CD) AR11554 (Cassette), Recorded: Studio

Deep Down South
Arbor Records AR11312 (CD) AR11314 (Cassette), Recorded: Studio

The Next Generation
Arbor Records AR11102 (CD) AR11104 (Cassette), Recorded: Studio

Todome
Arbor Records AR11802 (CD) AR11804 (Cassette), Recorded: studio

Spirit Mountain Singers
Much Respect
Arbor Records AR11224, Recorded: Studio, Format: Cassette

Spirit Sand Singers
Sacred Ground
Arbor Records AR11072, Recorded: Studio, Format: Cassette

Spirit Whistle
Round Dance
SWEET GRASS RECORDS (No Number), Recorded: Studio, Format: CD

Spirit Wind Singers
Spirit Wind Singers
SUNSHINE RECORDS SSCT 4256, Recorded: Studio, Format: Cassette

Star Blanket Jr's
Get Up and Dance
CANYON RECORDS CR-6268, Recorded: Studio, Format: Cassette

Stoney Creek
Schemitzun '97
SWEET GRASS RECORDS SGSC91998, Recorded: Live, Format: CD,
Cassette

Stoney Eagle
Stoney Eagle
SUNSHINE RECORDS SSCT 4143, Recorded: Studio, Format: Cassette

Stoney Eagle Round Dances
SUNSHINE RECORDS SSCT 4146, Recorded: Studio, Format: Cassette

Stoney Eagle Round Dance Songs Vol. III
SUNSHINE RECORDS SSCT 4209, Recorded: Studio, Format: Cassette

Stoney Eagle Cree Round Dances Vol. III
SUNSHINE RECORDS SSCT 4161, Recorded: Studio, Format: Cassette

Stoney Creek
Talking Eagle
Arbor Records AR11972, Recorded: Studio, Format: CD

Stoney Park Singers
Aude's Journey
SWEET GRASS RECORDS SGSP051494, Recorded: Studio, Format: CD

The Best of Stoney Park
SWEET GRASS RECORDS SGSP101699, Recorded: Studio, Format: CD,
Cassette

Don't Look Back
SWEET GRASS RECORDS SGSP062195, Recorded: Studio, Format: CD,
Cassette

Hartford '94
SWEET GRASS RECORDS SGSP019894, Recorded: Live, Format: Cassette

Looking for a Round Dance
SWEET GRASS RECORDS SGSP071496, Recorded: Studio, Format: Cassette

Posse
SWEET GRASS RECORDS SGSP071396, Recorded: Studio, Format: CD,
Cassette

Pow-Wow Songs
CANYON RECORDS CR-9014, Recorded: Studio, Format: Cassette

Schemitzun '95
SWEET GRASS RECORDS SGSP091495, Recorded: Live, Format: CD,
Cassette

Schemitzun '97
SWEET GRASS RECORDS SGSP90497, Recorded: Live, Format: CD,
Cassette

Stoney Park '93
SWEET GRASS RECORDS SP072893, Recorded: Studio, Format: Cassette

Wolf Pack
SWEET GRASS RECORDS SGSP81100, Recorded: Studio, Format: CD,
Cassette

Sweet Grass
Family Traditions
SWEET GRASS RECORDS SGSWEET GRASS RECORDS SG031696,
Recorded: Studio, Format: Cassette

Freedom
SWEET GRASS RECORDS SGS42099, Recorded: Studio, Format: Cassette

Honoring the Song
SWEET GRASS RECORDS SGSWEET GRASS RECORDS SG32297,
Recorded: Studio, Format: CD, Cassette

Ta-Otha Spirit
A Dream Takes Flight
SWEET GRASS RECORDS SGTS31498, Recorded: Studio, Format: CD,
Cassette

Tail Wind
Tail Wind
SUNSHINE RECORDS SSCT 4151, Recorded: Studio, Format: Cassette

Teton Rambler Jrs.
Teton Rambler Jrs.
SWEET GRASS RECORDS SGTR81596, Recorded: Studio, Format: Cassette

The Tootoosis Family
Vol.2, The Drums of Poundmaker
CANYON RECORDS CR-6157, Recorded: Studio, Format: Cassette

Thunder Horse
Native America
Arbor Records AR11592 (CD) AR11594 (Cassette), Recorded: Studio

Riding the Storm
Arbor Records AR11382 (CD) AR11384 (Cassette), Recorded: Studio

Thunder Mountain Singers
Ojibway Pow-Wow Songs
CANYON RECORDS CR-16225, Recorded: Studio, Format: Cassette

Thunder Mountain Singers
SUNSHINE RECORDS SSCT 4137, Recorded: Studio, Format: Cassette

Thunder Mountain Singers Vol. II
SUNSHINE RECORDS SSCT 4194, Recorded: Studio, Format: Cassette

Thunderchild, Vic
Thunderchild Singers
SUNSHINE RECORDS SSCT 4012, Recorded: Studio, Format: Cassette

Treaty 6 Ermine Skin
Pow-Wow Songs
CANYON RECORDS CR-6134, Recorded: Studio, Format: Cassette

Two Nations Singers
Round Dance Songs
CANYON RECORDS CR-9005, Recorded: Studio, Format: Cassette

UMOn Han Singers
The Dream
Arbor Records AR11214, Recorded: Studio, Format: Cassette

Various Artists
Anishinaabe Student Council 8th Gathering
SUNSHINE RECORDS SSCT 4255, Recorded: Live, Format: Cassette

Ann Arbor Pow Wow 1996
SUNSHINE RECORDS SSCT 4298, Recorded: Live, Format: Cassette

Best of Hinkley Pow Wow
Arbor Records AR11882 (CD) AR11884 (Cassette), Recorded: Live

Bismark Pow Wow
SUNSHINE RECORDS SSCT 4189, Recorded: Live, Format: Cassette

Blackfeet Grass Dance & Owl Dance Songs
INDIAN HOUSE RECORDS SC 104
Contents:12 grass dance songs, 6 owl dance songs
Singers: Edward Morning Owl, Wilbur Morning Owl
Recorded: at Cardston, Alberta, Canada, July 15, 1962
Tribe: Blackfeet
Format: Cassette

C.I.S. 20th Annual Pow Wow
SUNSHINE RECORDS SSCT 4172, Recorded: Live, Format: Cassette

Dakota Hotain Singers
SUNSHINE RECORDS SSCT 4059, Recorded: Studio, Format: Cassette

Eagle Butte Live
SUNSHINE RECORDS SSCT 4215, Recorded: Live, Format: Cassette

Eagle Butte Live Vol. II
SUNSHINE RECORDS SSCT 4218, Recorded: Live, Format: Cassette

Hearts of the Nations at Banff 97
SWEET GRASS RECORDS (No Number) , Recorded: Live, Format: CD, Cassette

Hertel Wisconsin Vol. I
SUNSHINE RECORDS SSCT 4234, Recorded: Live, Format: Cassette

Hertel Wisconsin Vol. II
SUNSHINE RECORDS SSCT 4235, Recorded: Live, Format: Cassette

Hinckley Hand Drum Songs Vol. I
SUNSHINE RECORDS SSCT 4241, Recorded: Live, Format: Cassette

Hinckley Hand Drum Songs Vol. II
SUNSHINE RECORDS SSCT 4242, Recorded: Live, Format: Cassette

Hinckley Northern Style
SUNSHINE RECORDS SSCT 4283, Recorded: Live, Format: Cassette

Hinkley Northern Style 1999
Arbor Records AR11162 (CD) AR11164 (Cassette), Recorded: Live

Hinckley Northern Style 2000
Arbor Records AR11412, Recorded: Live, Format: CD

Hinckley Southern Style
SUNSHINE RECORDS SSCT 4284, Recorded: Live, Format: Cassette

Hinkley Southern Style 1999
Arbor Records AR11152 (CD) AR11154 (Cassette), Recorded: Live
Hinkley Southern Style 2000
Arbor Records AR11422 (CD) AR11424 (Cassette), Recorded: Live

Hinckley Pow Wow Vol. I
SUNSHINE RECORDS SSCT 4243, Recorded: Live, Format: Cassette

Hinckley Pow Wow Vol. II
SUNSHINE RECORDS SSCT 4244, Recorded: Live, Format: Cassette

In Honor of Art Moosomin: Live Round Dance
SWEET GRASS RECORDS SGAM12100, Recorded: Live, Format: CD, Cassette

Indian Summer Fest: Thunder on the Lake
Arbor Records AR11982, Recorded: Live, Format: CD

Minnesota Pow Wow Songs
SUNSHINE RECORDS SSCT 4174, Recorded: Studio, Format: Cassette

Onion Lake Pow Wow '92
SUNSHINE RECORDS SSCT 4149, Recorded: Live, Format: Cassette

Pow Wow Legends
SUNSHINE RECORDS, Recorded: Studio, Format: CD SSCD4413, Tape
SSCT4413

Pow Wow Vol. I
SUNSHINE RECORDS SSCT 4286, Recorded: Live, Format: Cassette

Pow Wow Vol. II
SUNSHINE RECORDS SSCT 4287, Recorded: Live, Format: Cassette

St. Crioux 2nd Annual Pow Wow
SUNSHINE RECORDS SSCT 4217, Recorded: Live, Format: Cassette

St. Crioux 2nd Annual Pow Wow Vol. II
SUNSHINE RECORDS SSCT 4219, Recorded: Live, Format: Cassette

Schemitzun '99:Best of the Best '93-'99
SWEET GRASS RECORDS SGS91899, Recorded: Live, Format: CD, Cassette

Songs from the Battleford Pow Wow
CANYON RECORDS CR-6142, Recorded: Live, Format: Cassette

Spirit of the Nations
SUNSHINE RECORDS, Recorded: Studio, Format: CD SSCD4451, Tape
SSCT4451

The Sounds of Champions: Onion Lake '94
SWEET GRASS RECORDS SGOL072394, Recorded: Live, Format: Cassette

Thunder Bear Pow Wow
SUNSHINE RECORDS SSCT 4188, Recorded: Live, Format: Cassette

Thunder Drums Volume 1
Arbor Records AR11352, Recorded: Live, Format: CD

Thunder Drums Volume 2
Arbor Records AR11562 (CD) AR11564 (Cassette), Recorded: Live

Wisconsin Intertribals
SUNSHINE RECORDS SSCT 4216, Recorded: Live, Format: Cassette

White Earth 125th Pow Wow
SUNSHINE RECORDS SSCT 4173, Recorded: Live, Format: Cassette

White Earth 126th Pow Wow
SUNSHINE RECORDS SSCT 4222, Recorded: Live, Format: Cassette

World's Best Round Dance Vol. 1
SUNSHINE RECORDS, Recorded: Studio, Format: CD SSCD4317, Tape SSCT431

Walkin' Bull
Walkin' Bull
Arbor Records AR11602 (CD) AR11604 (Cassette), Recorded: Studio

Walking Buffalo
The Chase
SWEET GRASS RECORDS SGWB52397, Recorded: Studio, Format: CD, Cassette

Distant Voices
SWEET GRASS RECORDS SGWB032896, Recorded: Studio, Format: Cassette

Walking Buffalo '98
SWEET GRASS RECORDS SGWB1179, Recorded: Studio, Format: CD

Walking Wolf
Walking Wolf Singers, Vol 2
SUNSHINE RECORDS, Recorded: Studio, Format: CD SSCD4423, Tape SSCT4423

Wandering Sound Singers
Wandering Sound Singers
SUNSHINE RECORDS SSCT 4201, Recorded: Studio, Format: Cassette

White Eagle
White Eagle
SUNSHINE RECORDS SSCT 4186, Recorded: Studio, Format: Cassette

White Eagle Cloud
White Eagle Cloud
SUNSHINE RECORDS SSCT 4227, Recorded: Studio, Format: Cassette

White Lodge
The Next Generation
SWEET GRASS RECORDS SGWL82397, Recorded: Studio, Format: CD, Cassette

White Lodge
Arbor Records AR11332 (CD) AR11334 (Cassette), Recorded: Studio

White Ridge
White Ridge
SWEET GRASS RECORDS SGWR112695, Recorded: Studio, Format: Cassette

White Ridge Singers
SUNSHINE RECORDS SSCT 4246, Recorded: Studio, Format: Cassette

White Tail
For our Elders
Arbor Records AR11532 (CD) AR11534 (Cassette), Recorded: Studio

Live@ Hinckley
Arbopr Records AR11462 (CD) AR11464 (Cassette), Recorded: Live

White Whale Jrs.
White Whale Jrs.
SWEET GRASS RECORDS SGWW031294, Recorded: Studio, Format: Cassette

Whitefish Bay Singers
Pow Wow 2k
Arbor Records AR 11172 (CD) AR11174 (Cassette) Recorded: Studio

Ndoo to Mag
Arbor Records AR11022 (CD) AR11024 (Cassette), Recorded: Studio

White Fish Bay J.R. Tribute to Gabe White
SUNSHINE RECORDS SSCT 4206, Recorded: Studio, Format: Cassette

Whitefish Bay Compilation Pow Wow '92
SUNSHINE RECORDS SSCT 4145, Recorded: Live, Format: Cassette

Whitefish Bay Singers
SUNSHINE RECORDS SSBCT 4097, Recorded: Studio, Format: Cassette

Whitefish Bay Singers
SUNSHINE RECORDS SSCT 4116, Recorded: Studio, Format: Cassette

Whitefish Bay Singers, Volume 2
SUNSHINE RECORDS, Recorded: Studio, Format: CD SSCD4102, Tape SSCT4102

Whitefish Bay Singers Vol. VII
SUNSHINE RECORDS SSCT 4224, Recorded: Studio, Format: Cassette

Whitefish Bay Singers Vol. IV
SUNSHINE RECORDS SSCT 4134, Recorded: Studio, Format: Cassette

Whitefish Bay Singers Vol. V
SUNSHINE RECORDS SSCT 4153, Recorded: Studio, Format: Cassette

Whitefish Bay Singers Vol. VI
SUNSHINE RECORDS SSCT 4191, Recorded: Studio, Format: Cassette

Whitefish Jrs
Cree Man
SWEET GRASS RECORDS SGWF112500, Recorded: Studio, Format: CD, Cassette

Forever Dancing
SWEET GRASS RECORDS SGWF020295, Recorded: Studio, Format: Cassette

Hartford '94
SWEET GRASS RECORDS SGWF091794, Recorded: Live, Format: Cassette

In Honour of Percy Dreaver Round Dance
SWEET GRASS RECORDS SGWF010803, Recorded: Studio, Format: CD

Life Giver
SWEET GRASS RECORDS SGWF051296, Recorded: Studio, Format: CD, Cassette

Live at Batchewana
SWEET GRASS RECORDS SGWF9896, Recorded: Live, Format: CD, Cassette

Traditions
SWEET GRASS RECORDS SGWF030594, Recorded: Studio, Format: CD, Cassette

A Way of Life
SWEET GRASS RECORDS SGWF81498, Recorded: Studio, Format: CD, Cassette

World's Leading Round Dance Songs Volume I
SWEET GRASS RECORDS SGRD12596, Recorded: Studio, Format: CD

World's Leading Round Dance Songs Volume II
SWEET GRASS RECORDS SGRD11598, Recorded: Studio, Format: CD, Cassette

Wild Horse
Let it Ride
SWEET GRASS RECORDS SGWH60700, Recorded: Studio, Format: CD, Cassette

Wild Horse '99
SWEET GRASS RECORDS SGWH8199, Recorded: Studio, Format: CD, Cassette

Willow Creek
Veteran Songs, Recorded: Studio, Format: Cassette
SUNSHINE RECORDS SSCT 4211

Windy Rock Singers
Windy Rock Singers
SUNSHINE RECORDS SSCT 4166, Recorded: Studio, Format: Cassette

Wisconsin Dells
Schemitzun '95
SWEET GRASS RECORDS SGWD091795, Recorded: Live, Format: CD

Schemitzun '97
SWEET GRASS RECORDS SGWD90697, Recorded: Live, Format: CD, Cassette

Ya_Iyo_Waza
Ya_Iyo_Waza
SUNSHINE RECORDS SSCT 4214, Recorded: Studio, Format: Cassette

Yellowbird
Elite
Arbor Records AR11902, Recorded: Studio, Format: CD

Young Grey Horse
The Vibez
Arbor Records AR11592 (CD) AR11584 (Cassette), Recorded: Studio

TP Creepin'
Arbor Records AR11302, Recorded: Studio, Format: CD

Young Scouts
Meet Ya at the Round Dance
SWEET GRASS RECORDS SGYSCD101002, Recorded: Studio, Format: CD

Zotigh
Schemitzun '98
SWEET GRASS RECORDS SGZ92098, Recorded: Studio, Format: CD, Cassette

Northern Pow Wow Groups

Ashland Singers
Northern Cheyenne War Dance
INDIAN HOUSE RECORDS 4201
Contents: 10 war dance songs
Singers: Daniel Foote, Laforce Lonebear, Henry Sioux, Corlett Teeth, Harvey
Whiteman, Oran C. Wolfblack, Wesley Wolf Black
Recorded: at Lame Deer, Montana, May 12, 1974
Tribe: Northern Cheyenne
Format: Cassette, LP

Bad Canyon Wellpinit
Pow-Wow Songs
CANYON RECORDS CR-6174, Recorded: Studio, Format: Cassette

Badland Singers
Assiniboine-Sioux Grass Dance
INDIAN HOUSE RECORDS 4101
Contents: 10 grass dance songs
Singers: Lyle E. Denny, Rusty Denny, Gary Drum, Ben G. Hawk, Gerald
Lambert, Gary Red Eagle, Adrian C. Spotted Bird Sr., Leland Spotted Bird
Recorded: at Poplar, Montana, May 8, 1974
Tribe: Assiniboine-Sioux
Format: Cassette, LP

Sounds of the Badland Singers
INDIAN HOUSE RECORDS 4102
Contents: 10 grass dance songs
Singers: Roy A. Azure III, Mathew Big Talk, Russell Denny, Gary Drum, Ben
Gray Hawk, Gerald R. Lambert, Adrian Spotted Bird, Leland Spotted Bird
Recorded: at Poplar, Montana, August 27, 1975
Tribe: Assiniboine-Sioux
Format: Cassette

Live at Bismarck
INDIAN HOUSE RECORDS 4103
Contents: 4 traditional honoring songs, 4 grass dance songs, 1 kahomini song, 1
round dance song
Singers: Mathew Big Talk, Rusty Denny, Gary Drum, Ben Gray Hawk, Gerald R.
Lambert, Adrian Spotted Bird, Leland Spotted Bird, Donald White Bear
Recorded: live at the 6th Annual United Tribes Days International Championship
Dancing and Singing Contest at Bismarck, North Dakota, September 5-7,1975
Tribe: Assiniboine-Sioux
Format: Cassette

The Badland Singers at Home
INDIAN HOUSE RECORDS 4104
Contents: 10 grass dance songs
Singers: Bradley Buffalo Calf, Russell Denny, Gary Drum, Ben Gray Hawk, Earl Jones Jr., Bill Runsabove, George Squirrel Coat, Mike G. Talks Different, Donald P. White Bear
Recorded: at Brockton, Montana, June 10, 1978
Tribe: Assiniboine-Sioux
Format: Cassette, LP

Kahomini Songs
INDIAN HOUSE RECORDS 4105
Contents: 10 kahomini songs (similar to owl dance)
Singers: Bradley Buffalo Calf, Lyle E. Denny, Russell Denny, Gary Drum, Ben Gray Hawk, Earl Jones Jr., Bill Runsabove, George Squirrel Coat, Mike G. Talks Different, Donald P. White Bear.
Recorded: at Brockton, Montana, June 11, 1978.
Tribe: Assiniboine-Sioux
Format: Cassette, LP

Live at United Tribes - Volume 1
INDIAN HOUSE RECORDS 4106
Contents: 5 grass dance songs, 5 traditional war songs
Singers: Roy A. Azure III, Lyle E. Denny, Russell Denny, Gary Drum, Ben Gray Hawk, Gerald R. Lambert, Bill Runsabove, Chuck Spotted Bird Sr., Leland Spotted Bird, George Squirrel Coat
Recorded: live at Dancing and Singing Contest at Bismarck, North Dakota, September 7-9, 1979
Tribe: Assiniboine-Sioux
Format: Cassette

Live at United Tribes - Volume 2
INDIAN HOUSE RECORDS 4107
Contents: 6 grass dance songs, 4 traditional war songs
Singers: Roy A. Azure III, Lyle E. Denny, Russell Denny, Gary Drum, Ben Gray Hawk, Gerald R. Lambert, Bill Runsabove, Chuck Spotted Bird Sr., Leland Spotted Bird, George Squirrel Coat
Recorded: live at the 10th Anniversary United Tribes Days International Championship Dancing and Singing Contest at Bismarck, North Dakota, September 7-9. 1979--Continued from INDIAN HOUSE RECORDS 4106
Tribe: Assiniboine-Sioux
Format: Cassette

Live at Santa Fe
INDIAN HOUSE RECORDS 4109
Contents: Honor song, 6 grass dance songs, 3 jingle dress songs, kahomini song, Nathan Crazy Bull flag song, Air Force veterans' song
Singers: Seymour Eagle Speaker, Bill Runsabove, Delray Smith, Chuck Spotted Bird, Merle Tendoy, Harry Three Stars Jr.
Recorded: live at the 4th Annual Santa Fe Powwow at Pojoaque Pueblo, New Mexico, May 27-30, 1994
Tribe: Assiniboine-Sioux
Format: CD, Cassette
Notes: The Badland Singers are a traditional singing group from Brockton, Montana, and have been singing together for more than 20 years. They have sung throughout the U.S. and Canada, winning awards in many singing competitions. They follow the original way of singing handed down by their elders, and provide outstanding Northern Plains style singing wherever they go. In this, their eighth recording, the Badland Singers present an outstanding variety of both old and new songs in their exciting singing style. Background notes on the songs are provided by the singers.

Black Lodge Singers

Blacklodge Singers
SUNSHINE RECORDS SSCT 4176, Recorded: Studio, Format: Cassette

Blacklodge Singers
SUNSHINE RECORDS SSCT 4150, Recorded: Studio, Format: Cassette

Pow Wow Highway Songs
SOAR 125, Recorded: Studio, Format: CD, Cassette

Pow Wow People
SOAR 150, Recorded: Studio, Format: CD, Cassette

Vol.1, Pow-Wow Songs
CANYON RECORDS CR-6195, Recorded: Studio, Format: Cassette

Vol.2, Pow-Wow Recorded Live
CANYON RECORDS CR-6202, Recorded: Live, Format: Cassette

Vol.3, Pow-Wow Recorded Live
CANYON RECORDS CR-6203, Recorded: Live, Format: Cassette

Vol.4, Intertribal Pow-Wow Songs
CANYON RECORDS CR-6204, Recorded: Studio, Format: Cassette

Vol.5, Intertribal Pow-Wow Songs
CANYON RECORDS CR-6208, Recorded: Studio, Format: Cassette

Vol.6, Live at Fort Duchesne
CANYON RECORDS CR-16209, Recorded: Live, Format: Cassette

Vol.7, Pow-Wow Songs
CANYON RECORDS CR-16213, Recorded: Studio, Format: Cassette

Vol.8, Veterans' Honor Songs
CANYON RECORDS CR-16214, Recorded: Studio, Format: Cassette

Vol.9, Pow-Wow Songs
CANYON RECORDS CR-16215, Recorded: Studio, Format: Cassette

Vol.10, Round Dance Songs
CANYON RECORDS CR-16216, Recorded: Studio, Format: Cassette

Vol.11, Pow Wow Songs
CANYON RECORDS CR-16271, Recorded: Studio, Format: Cassette

Vol.12, Intertribal Songs
CANYON RECORDS CR-16272, Recorded: Studio, Format: Cassette

Vol.13, Live at White Swan
CANYON RECORDS CR-6273, Recorded: Live, Format: Cassette

Vol.14, Kids' Pow-Wow Songs
CANYON RECORDS CR-6274, Recorded: Studio, Format: Cassette

Vol.15, Enter the Circle
CANYON RECORDS CR-6276, Recorded: Studio, Format: Cassette

Vol.16, Round Dance Tonight!
CANYON RECORDS CR-6278, Recorded: Studio, Format: Cassette

Vol.17, The People Dance
CANYON RECORDS CR-6293, Recorded: Studio, Format: Cassette

Vol. 18, Tribute to the Elders
CANYON RECORDS CR-6318, Recorded: Studio, Format: Cassette

Vol. 19, Weasel Tail's Dream
CANYON RECORDS CR-6337, Recorded: Studio, Format: Cassette

Vol. 20, It's Been a Long Time Comin'
CANYON RECORDS CR-6338, Recorded: Studio, Format: Cassette

Two World Concerto
CANYON RECORDS CR-7016, Recorded: Studio, Format: Cassette

Blackfeet Singers
Old Blackfeet Pow Wow Songs
CANYON RECORDS CR-6119, Recorded: Studio, Format: Cassette

Grayhorse Singers
Shake It Up
SOAR 148, Recorded: Studio, Format: CD, Cassette

Haystack Ramblers
Songs from Rocky Boy Pow-Wow
CANYON RECORDS CR-6104, Recorded: Studio, Format: Cassette

Heart Butte Singers
Vol.1, Pow-Wow Songs
CANYON RECORDS CR-6177, Recorded: Studio, Format: Cassette

Vol.2, Pow-Wow Songs
CANYON RECORDS CR-6187, Recorded: Studio, Format: Cassette

High Noon
Songs for our People
CANYON RECORDS CR-6355, Recorded: Studio, Format: Cassette

Ho Hwo Sju Lakota Singers
Traditional Songs of the Sioux
INDIAN HOUSE RECORDS 4301
Contents: Sioux national anthem, veteran's honor song, 3 grass dance songs, 2 flag dance songs, 2 rabbit dance songs
Singers: Franklin Bear Running, Romanus Bear Stops, Berdell Blue Arm, Steve Charging Eagle, Kenneth Young Bear, Zona Bear Stops, Lorraine Charging Eagle, Darlene Young Bear
Recorded: at Red Scaffold, South Dakota, May 16, 1974
Tribe: Lakota Sioux
Format: Cassette

Indian Creek Singers
Pow Wow Jams
SOAR 156, Recorded: Studio, Format: CD, Cassette

Pow Wow Season
SOAR 146, Recorded: Studio, Format: CD, Cassette

Ironwood Singers

Traditional Songs of the Sioux - Live at Rosebud Fair
INDIAN HOUSE RECORDS 4321
Contents: 11 traditional Lakota Sioux songs
Singers: Ben Blackbear Sr., Kenny Haukass, Harvey Larvie, Ernie Running,
David White, Ervin Yellow Robe
Recorded: live at The 102nd Rosebud Fair Wacipi, Rosebud, South Dakota,
August 25-27, 1978
Tribe: Lakota Sioux
Format: CD, Cassette
Notes: The Ironwood Singers are a traditional Lakota singing group from
Rosebud, South Dakota. They can sing many types of songs, but their specialty
is traditional songs. The group is well-known for its ability to sing exactly the right
song for a particular occasion, and to sing it well. Background notes and
translations of the Lakota lyrics are provided by the singers.

Live at The 106th Rosebud Sioux Fair
INDIAN HOUSE RECORDS 4322
Contents: 15 traditional war dance, grass dance, and contest songs
Singers: Harold Condon, Kenny Haukass, Robert Kim King, Harvey Larvie, Stan
Pretty Paint, Ernie Ray Running, George Whirlwind Soldier, Dave White, Sandra
Blackbear White
Recorded: live at Rosebud, South Dakota, August 28-30, 1982
Tribe: Lakota Sioux
Format: Cassette

Kicking Woman Singers

Vol.1, Intertribal Pow-Wow Songs
CANYON RECORDS CR-6178, Recorded: Studio, Format: Cassette

Vol.2, Pow-Wow Songs
CANYON RECORDS CR-6181, Recorded: Studio, Format: Cassette

Vol.3, Contest and Intertribal Songs
CANYON RECORDS CR-6183, Recorded: Studio, Format: Cassette

Vol.4, Intertribal Pow-Wow Songs
CANYON RECORDS CR-6200, Recorded: Studio, Format: Cassette

Vol.5, Pow-Wow Recorded Live!
CANYON RECORDS CR-6201, Recorded: Live, Format: Cassette

Vol.6, Pow-Wow Songs
CANYON RECORDS CR-16223, Recorded: Studio, Format: Cassette

Vol.7, Intertribal Pow-Wow Songs
CANYON RECORDS CR-16224, Recorded: Studio, Format: Cassette

Vol.8, Pow-Wow Songs
CANYON RECORDS CR-16253, Recorded: Studio, Format: Cassette

Vol.9, Our Way of Life
CANYON RECORDS CR-6299, Recorded: Studio, Format: Cassette

Vol. 10, Pikuni Style
CANYON RECORDS CR-6333, Recorded: Studio, Format: Cassette

Little Corner Singers
Pow-Wow Songs
CANYON RECORDS CR-6189, Recorded: Studio, Format: Cassette

Mandaree Singers
Vol.2, Pow-Wow Songs
CANYON RECORDS CR-8002, Recorded: Studio, Format: Cassette

MGM Singers
Intertribal Pow-Wow Songs
CANYON RECORDS CR-16244, Recorded: Studio, Format: Cassette

Northern Plains Society Singers
Northern Plains Society Singers
CANYON RECORDS CR-6122, Recorded: Studio, Format: Cassette

Omak Pow Wow
CANYON RECORDS CR-6175, Recorded: Live, Format: Cassette

1993 Hinkley Grand Celebration
CANYON RECORDS CR-16263, Recorded: Live, Format: Cassette

Parker Singers
Vol.1, Cree Pow-Wow Songs
CANYON RECORDS CR-6091, Recorded: Studio, Format: Cassette

Vol.2, Cree Pow-Wow Songs
CANYON RECORDS CR-8031, Recorded: Studio, Format: Cassette

Plains Indian Singers
Pow-Wow Songs
CANYON RECORDS CR-16255, Recorded: Studio, Format: Cassette

Crow Celebration
CANYON RECORDS CR-6089, Recorded: Live, Format: Cassette

Kyi Yo Pow-Wow
CANYON RECORDS CR-6111, Recorded: Live, Format: Cassette

Red Earth Singers
Live at Bismarck
INDIAN HOUSE RECORDS 4501
Contents: Grand entry song, 8 war dance songs, trick contest song
Singers: Homer Bear Jr., Edward Bearheart Jr., Keith Davenport, Gerald McMaster, Adrian Pushetonequa, Wayne Pushetonequa, Richard K. Rice, Dean Whitebreast
Recorded: live at the 6th Annual United Tribes Days International Championship Dancing and Singing Contest at Bismarck, North Dakota, September 5-7, 1975
Tribe: Mesquakie
Format: Cassette

Red Earth Singers
INDIAN HOUSE RECORDS 4502
Contents: Grand entry song, flag song, 6 war dance songs
Singers: Edward Bearheart, Vince Beyl, Keith Davenport, Stony Larson, Adrian Pushetonequa, Wayne Pushetonequa, Dean Whitebreast
Recorded: at Tama, Iowa, June 3, 1978
Tribe: Mesquakie
Format: Cassette

Red Earth Singers Of Tama, Iowa - Live
INDIAN HOUSE RECORDS 4503
Contents: 2 grand entry songs, 6 intertribal songs, shake song
Singers: Wayne Pushetonequa, Adrian Pushetonequa, Keith Davenport, Mike S. Sanache, Quinton Pushetonequa, Brenton Pushetonequa, Martel Pushetonequa
Recorded: live at the 6th Annual Taos Pueblo Powwow, Taos, New Mexico, July 13-15, 1990
Tribe: Mesquakie
Format: Cassette

Rocky Boy
Chippewa-Cree Grass Dance Songs
INDIAN HOUSE RECORDS 4401
Contents: 10 Chippewa-Cree grass dance songs
Singers: Charles Gopher, John Meyers, Duncan Standing Rock, Lloyd Top Sky, Henry Wolfchild
Recorded: at Rocky Boy, Montana, May 29, 1980
Tribe: Chippewa-Cree
Format: Cassette

Grass Dance and Jingle Dress Songs - Volume 1
INDIAN HOUSE RECORDS 4402
Contents: 5 grass dance songs, 5 jingle dress songs
Singers: Charles Gopher, Jonathan Gopher, Kenneth Gopher, Robert Taylor, Merle Tendoy Sr., Lloyd Top Sky
Recorded: at Rocky Boy, Montana, September 3, 1992
Tribe: Chippewa-Cree
Format: Cassette

Grass Dance & Jingle Dress Songs - Volume 2
INDIAN HOUSE RECORDS 4403
Contents: 4 grass dance songs, 6 jingle dress songs
Singers: Charles Gopher, Jonathan Gopher, Kenneth Gopher, Robert Taylor, Merle Tendoy Sr., Lloyd Top Sky
Recorded: at Rocky Boy, Montana, September 3, 1992--Continued from INDIAN HOUSE RECORDS 4402
Tribe: Chippewa-Cree
Format: Cassette

Rocky Boys
Vol.2, Pow-Wow Songs
CANYON RECORDS CR-6154, Recorded: Studio, Format: Cassette

Sage Point Singers
Pow Wow Cookin'
SOAR 119, Recorded: Studio, Format: CD, Cassette

Selam & Hill
Pow-Wow Songs Recorded Live!
CANYON RECORDS CR-6173, Recorded: Live, Format: Cassette

Spotted Eagle Singers
Intertribal Pow-Wow Songs
CANYON RECORDS CR-6190, Recorded: Studio, Format: Cassette

Two Medicine Lake Singers
Vol.1, Pow-Wow Songs
CANYON RECORDS CR-6176, Recorded: Studio, Format: Cassette

Vol. 2, Grass Dance Songs
CANYON RECORDS CR-6182, Recorded: Studio, Format: Cassette

Various Artists
Blackfeet Grass Dance Songs
INDIAN HOUSE RECORDS SC 100
Contents: 11 grass dance songs
Singers: Allen White Grass, Pat Kennedy, Stanley Whiteman
Recorded: at Browning, Montana, July 2, 1960
Tribe: Blackfeet
Format: Cassette

Chippewa-Cree Grass Dance
INDIAN HOUSE RECORDS SC 101
Contents: 14 grass dance songs
Singers: 'Rocky Boy Singers' Paul Eagleman, Charles Gopher, Bill Baker, John Gilbert Meyers, Windy Boy
Recorded: at Crow Agency, Montana, August 22, 1966
Tribe: Chippewa-Cree
Format: Cassette

Gathering of Nations Pow Wow
SOAR 133, Recorded: Live, Format: CD, Cassette

Gathering of Nations Pow Wow '92
SOAR 144, Recorded: Live, Format: CD, Cassette

Gathering of Nations Pow Wow '93
SOAR 158, Recorded: Live, Format: CD, Cassette

Gathering of Nations Pow Wow '99
SOAR, Recorded: Live, Format: CD, Cassette

Gathering of Nations Pow Wow 2000
SOAR, Recorded: Live, Format: CD, Cassette

Northern Cheyenne Warriors Dance and Crow Tribal Grass Dance Songs
INDIAN HOUSE RECORDS SC 112
Contents: 6 Northern Cheyenne warrior dance songs, 7 Crow grass dance songs
Singers: Phillip Whiteman, Gilbert White Dirt, Thomas Wooden Leg, James Red Cloud, Henry Old Coyote, Lloyd Old Coyote, Warren Bear Cloud, John Strong Enemy
Tribe: Northern Cheynne, Crow
Format: Cassette

Crow Grass and Owl Dance Songs
INDIAN HOUSE RECORDS SC 116
Contents: 12 grass dance songs, 4 owl dance songs
Singers: Lloyd Old Coyote, Frank Backbone, Sr., Robert Other Medicine, Lindsey Bad Bear, Warren Bear Cloud, John Strong Enemy
Recorded: at Crow Agency, Montana
Tribe: Crow
Format: Cassette

Menominee and Winnebago Tribal Songs
INDIAN HOUSE RECORDS SC 117
Contents: 10 Winnebago war dance songs, 6 Menominee womenÕs dance songs, Winnebago tribal greeting song, Chief Song, Air Raid on Iwo Jima, Korean War song
Singers: John Awonohopay, Howard Raine, Winslow White Eagle
Recorded: at Wisconsin Dells, WI, March 1, 1956.
Tribe: Menominee and Winnebago
Format: Cassette

Chippewa-Cree Circle Dance
INDIAN HOUSE RECORDS SC 200
Contents: 13 circle dance songs
Singers: "Rocky Boy Singers": Paul Eagleman, Charles Gopher, Bill Baker, John Gilbert Meyers, Windy Boy
Recorded: at Crow Agency, Montana, August 22, 1966
Tribe: Chippewa-Cree
Format: Cassette

White Earth Pow-Wow (1979)
CANYON RECORDS CR-6171 Format: Cassette

White Eagle Singers
Vol.1, Intertribal Pow-Wow Songs
CANYON RECORDS CR-6185, Recorded: Studio, Format: Cassette

Vol.2, Intertribal Pow-Wow Songs
CANYON RECORDS CR-6186, Recorded: Studio, Format: Cassette

Vol.3., Intertribal Pow-Wow Songs
CANYON RECORDS CR-6197, Recorded: Studio, Format: Cassette

Vol.4, Round Dance & Love Songs
CANYON RECORDS CR-6198, Recorded: Studio, Format: Cassette

Vol.5, Pow-Wow Song
CANYON RECORDS CR-6199, Recorded: Studio, Format: Cassette

Vol.6, Fifth Generation
CANYON RECORDS CR-16235, Recorded: Studio, Format: Cassette

"Get Up & Dance" - Pow-Wow Songs
CANYON RECORDS CR-6266, Recorded: Studio, Format: Cassette

Vol.2, Recorded Live at the U. of A.
CANYON RECORDS CR-6267, Recorded: Live, Format: Cassette

Keepin' It Real
CANYON RECORDS CR-6298, Recorded: Studio, Format: Cassette

Thunder & Lightning
CANYON RECORDS CR-6339, Recorded: Studio, Format: Cassette

Drum for Life
CANYON RECORDS CR-6349, Recorded: Studio, Format: Cassette

White Thunder
Vol.1, Potawatami Pow-Wow Songs
CANYON RECORDS CR-16261 Tribe: Potawatami, Recorded: Studio, Format: Cassette

Vol.2, Potawatami Pow-Wow Songs
CANYON RECORDS CR-16262 Tribe: Potawatami, Recorded: Studio, Format: Cassette

Young Grey Horse
Generations
CANYON RECORDS CR-6286, Recorded: Studio, Format: Cassette

Starting Young
SOAR 155, Recorded: Studio, Format: CD, Cassette

Yampakira Singers
Pow Wow Jams
SOAR 156, Recorded: Studio, Format: CD, Cassette

Young Grey Horse Society
Vol.1, Songs of the Blackfeet
CANYON RECORDS CR-6164, Recorded: Studio, Format: Cassette

Vol.2, Pow-Wow Songs
CANYON RECORDS CR-6184, Recorded: Studio, Format: Cassette

Vol.3, Pow-Wow Songs
CANYON RECORDS CR-6193, Recorded: Studio, Format: Cassette

Southern Pow Wow Groups

Fort Oakland Ramblers
Oklahoma Intertribal and Contest Songs
INDIAN HOUSE RECORDS IH 2015
Contents: Ponca flag song, 6 intertribal songs, 2 patriotic give-away songs, 4
contest songs, Ponca veterans' song
Singers: Perry Lee Botone Jr., Jim Grant, James Kemble, Garland Kent Jr.,
Gregory Lieb, Oliver Little Cook, Stephen Little Cook, Don Patterson, Henry
Patterson, Jade R. Roubedeaux, Sophina Buffalohead, Tesa Goodeagle,
Roberta J. McIntosh, Dobbin Monoessy
Recorded at: White Eagle, Oklahoma, March 21,1992
Tribe: Ponca, Otoe, Intertribal
Format: Cassette

Rose Hill
Live at Hinckley
INDIAN HOUSE RECORDS IH 2101
Contents: Sac and Fox flag song, 9 intertribal songs
Singers: Lloyd Gwin, Junior Whitecloud, Michael Whitecloud, Roland Barker,
Hootie Whitecloud, Curtis Hamilton, Juaquin Hamilton, Henry Walker Jr., Brian
Frejo, Donnie Hamilton, R.G. Harris, Greg Victors, Shude Victors
Recorded live at: the Mille Lacs Band Of Ojibwe 4th Annual Grand Celebration,
Hinckley, Minnesota, July 28-30, 1995
Tribe: Sac & Fox, Intertribal
Format: CD, Cassette
Additional information: The Rose Hill Singers are a group of young men from the
Sac and Fox and Otoe tribes of north central Oklahoma. In the past few years,
Rose Hill has become well-known throughout the U.S. and Canada for their
many intertribal songs and strong singing style. This album presents an
outstanding performance, for which Rose Hill was awarded first place in the
Southern Plains singing competition at the Mille Lacs Band of Ojibwe Grand
Celebration at Hinckley, Minnesota.

Southern Thunder
Intertribal Songs Of Oklahoma
INDIAN HOUSE RECORDS IH 2081
Contents: Osage flag song, 14 intertribal songs, 2 Pawnee veterans' songs,
Pawnee war dance song
Singers: Frank M. Adson, Herb Adson, Kenny Bighorse Jr., Scott Bighorse, Vann
Bighorse, Larry Cozad, Scott George, Oliver Little Cook, George L. Valliere,
Chris White, Charlene Cozad, Mary George, Tesa Goodeagle, Andrea Kemble,
Linda Lazelle, Georgia Tiger
Recorded at: Hominy, Oklahoma, March 23, 1992
Tribe: Pawnee, Osage, Intertribal
Format: Cassette

Reachin' Out
INDIAN HOUSE RECORDS IH 2082
Contents: 14 intertribal songs, individual song, appreciation song
Singers: Frank M. Adson, Herb Adson, Kenny Bighorse Jr., Scott Bighorse, Vann Bighorse, Larry Cozad, George, George L. Valliere, Chris White, Mary Bighorse, Summer Bighorse, Charlene Cozad, Mary George, Tesa Goodeagle, Andrea Kemble, Lind a Lazelle, Georgia Tiger
Recorded at: Hominy, Oklahoma, April 26, 1993
Tribe: Pawnee, Osage, Intertribal
Format: Cassette

From The Heart - Volume 1
INDIAN HOUSE RECORDS IH 2083
Contents: 7 intertribal songs, Pawnee song, Angela Thurman's song
Singers: Frank Adson, Herb Adson, Kenny Bighorse Jr., Vann Bighorse, Joe Cozad, Kenneth L. Cozad, Scott George, Chris C. White, Byron Wichita, Kim Adson, Mary G. Bighorse, Summer Bighorse, Georgia Tiger, Julia F. Tiger
Recorded live at: the Keh-Wit Taspa Spring Celebration, Cabazon Reservation, California, March 24-26, 1995
Tribe: Intertribal, Pawnee
Format: CD, Cassette
Additional information: Southern Thunder is comprised of men and women from the Pawnee, Osage, Sac and Fox, and Shawnee tribes. The variety of tribes represented in the group provides them with an unusually large repertoire of songs. The exceptionally strong women singers has made Southern Thunder widely known for their distinctive sound, reminiscent of a multi-part orchestra. This album, recorded live in March, 1995, was one of those rare, fortunate times when an outstanding performance and a high quality digital recorder got together.

From The Heart - Volume 2
INDIAN HOUSE RECORDS IH 2084
Contents: Kenneth Goodeagle's song, 6 Pawnee songs, 2 intertribal songs, appreciation song
Singers: Frank Adson, Herb Adson, Kenny Bighorse Jr., Vann Bighorse, Joe Cozad, Kenneth L. Cozad, Scott George, Chris C. White, Byron Wichita, Kim Adson, Mary G. Bighorse, Summer Bighorse, Georgia Tiger, Julia F. Tiger
Recorded live at: the Keh-Wit Taspa Spring Celebration, Cabazon Reservation, California, March 24-26, 1995--Continued from INDIAN HOUSE RECORDS IH 2083
Tribe: Intertribal, Pawnee
Format: Cassette

O-Ho-Mah Lodge Singers
War Dance Songs Of The Kiowa - Volume 1
INDIAN HOUSE RECORDS IH 2508
Contents: 17 traditional Kiowa war dance songs
Singers: Ralph Kotay, Dixon Palmer, Rusty Wahkinney, Bill Ware, Tom Ware, Truman Ware, Mac Whitehorse, Mildred Kotay, Maxine Wahkinney, Florene Whitehorse, Lucille Whitehorse
Recorded at: Anadarko, Oklahoma, June 4, 1975
Tribe: Kiowa Format: Cassette

War Dance Songs Of The Kiowa - Volume 2
INDIAN HOUSE RECORDS IH 2509
Contents: 17 traditional Kiowa war dance songs (including contest songs and O-Ho-Mah quitting song)
Singers: Ralph Kotay, Dixon Palmer, Rusty Wahkinney, Bill Ware, Tom Ware, Truman Ware, Mac Whitehorse, Mildred Kotay, Maxine Wahkinney, Florene Whitehorse, Lucille Whitehorse
Recorded at: Anadarko, Oklahoma, June 4, 1975 Continued from INDIAN HOUSE RECORDS IH 2508
Tribe: Kiowa
Format: Cassette, LP

Various Artists
Chippewa-Cree Circle Dance
INDIAN HOUSE RECORDS SC 200 Contents: 13 circle dance songs
Singers: "Rocky Boy Singers": Paul Eagleman, Charles Gopher, Bill Baker, John Gilbert Meyers, Windy Boy
Recorded: Crow Agency, Montana, August 22, 1966
Tribe: Chippewa-Cree
Format: Cassette

Kiowa Circle & Two-Step Songs
INDIAN HOUSE RECORDS SC 278
Contents: 12 round dance songs
Singers: Leonard Cozad, Jasper Sankadota, Oscar Tahlo, Laura Tahlo
Recorded at: Carnegie, Oklahoma, January 22, 1964
Tribe: Kiowa
Format: Cassette

Kiowa Gourd Dance - Volume 1
INDIAN HOUSE RECORDS IH 2503
Contents: 12 Kiowa gourd dance songs
Singers: Daniel Cozad, Joe Cozad, Larry Cozad, Leonard Cozad Sr., Billy Hunting Horse, Adam Kaulaity, Vincent Spotted Bird, Yale Spotted Bird, Velma Cozad, Barbara Ahhaitty Monoessy, Dobbin Monoessy, Naomi Svitak Dancers are David Apekaum, Marty Autaubo, Richard Kauahquo, Elrod Monoessy, Curtis Tointigh
Recorded at: Carnegie, Oklahoma, June 10, 1974
Tribe: Kiowa
Format: CD, Cassette

Kiowa Gourd Dance - Volume 2
INDIAN HOUSE RECORDS IH 2504
Contents: 11 Kiowa gourd dance songs
Singers: Daniel Cozad, Joe Cozad, Larry Cozad, Leonard Cozad Sr., Billy Hunting Horse, Adam Kaulaity, Vincent Spotted Bird, Yale Spotted Bird, Velma Cozad, Barbara Ahhaitty Monoessy, Dobbin Monoessy, Naomi Svitak Dancers are David Apekaum, Marty Autaubo, Richard Kauahquo, Elrod Monoessy, Curtis Tointigh
Recorded at: Carnegie, Oklahoma, June 10, 1974--Continued from INDIAN HOUSE RECORDS IH 2503 Tribe: Kiowa Format: Cassette

Kiowa 49 - War Expedition Songs
INDIAN HOUSE RECORDS IH 2505
Contents: 17 Kiowa "49" songs
Singers: Gregory Haumpy, Billy Hunting Horse, Ralph Kotay, Bill Koomsa Jr.,
Barbara Ahhaitty, Pearl Kerche, Angeline Koomsa, Nan B. Koomsa, Wilda
Koomsa
Recorded at: Carnegie, Oklahoma, April 29, 1969
Tribe: Kiowa
Format: Cassette, LP

Kiowa Warriors Dance Songs and War Expedition ("49") Songs
INDIAN HOUSE RECORDS SC 131
Contents: 8 Kiowa warriors dance songs, 7 Kiowa war expedition ("49") songs
Singers: "The Soundchief Singers": James Aunguoe, Nathan Doyebi, Ernest Red
Bird, Ruth Red Bird
Tribe: Kiowa
Format: Cassette

Ponca Tribal Songs
INDIAN HOUSE RECORDS SC 119
Contents: Ponca flag song, veterans' song, memorial song, 3 trot dance songs, 7
war dance songs, 4 contest songs
Singers: Lamont Brown, Sylvester Warrior, Albert Waters, Henry Snake
Recorded: August 25 and 27, 1967
Tribe: Ponca
Format: Cassette

Ponca Warriors Dance Songs and Pawnee Warriors Dance Songs
INDIAN HOUSE RECORDS SC 118
Contents: 10 Ponca warriors dance songs, Pawnee flag song, 12 Pawnee
warriors dance songs
Singers: Sylvester Warrior, Albert Waters, Francis Eagle, Frank Murrie, Lamont
Pratt, Phillip Jim, Mrs. Jacob Leader
Tribe: Ponca, Pawnee
Format: Cassette

War Dance Songs Of The Ponca - Volume 1
INDIAN HOUSE RECORDS IH 2001
Contents: 18 war dance songs of the Ponca Hethoshka
Singers: Lamont Brown, Harry Buffalohead, Joe H. Rush, Russell Rush,
Sylvester Warrior, Albert Waters, Louis Yellow Horse, Alice Cook, Lucy C.F.
Ribs, Stella Yellow Horse.
Camp Crier: James Waters
Recorded at: Ponca City, Oklahoma, May 15, 1967
Tribe: Ponca
Format: Cassette

War Dance Songs Of The Ponca - Volume 2
INDIAN HOUSE RECORDS IH 2002
Contents: 22 war dance songs of the Ponca Hethoshka (including trot songs and charging songs)
Singers: Lamont Brown, Harry Buffalohead, Joe H. Rush, Russell Rush, Sylvester Warrior, Albert Waters, Louis Yellow Horse, Alice Cook, Lucy C.F. Ribs, Stella Yellow Horse
Camp Crier: James Waters--Continued from INDIAN HOUSE RECORDS IH 2001
Tribe: Ponca
Format: Cassette

Yellowhammer
Live at Hollywood, Florida
INDIAN HOUSE RECORDS IH 2016
Contents: Otoe flag song and victory song, Ponca flag song and contest songs, 7 intertribal songs
Singers: Perry Lee Botone Jr., Mike Gawhega, Jim Grant, Wesley J. Hudson, James Kemble, Garland Kent Jr., Gregory Lieb, Kinsel Lieb, John McIntosh
Recorded live at: at the 24th Annual Seminole Tribal Powwow at Hollywood, Florida, February 9-12, 1995
Tribe: Ponca, Otoe, Intertribal
Format: CD, Cassette
Additional information:Yellowhammer is a traditional Southern Plains style singing group from north central Oklahoma. The group consists of members of the Ponca and Otoe-Missouria tribes of Oklahoma. Since 1992, Yellowhammer has sung at powwows throughout the United States. The group has quickly become known for their excellent repertoire of traditional Ponca and Otoe songs, as well as their many new intertribal compositions. In 1995, Yellowhammer won first place in the Southern Plains singing competition at Schemitzun '95, the world's largest competition powwow.

Red Rock, Oklahoma
INDIAN HOUSE RECORDS IH 2017
Contents: 10 intertribal songs
Singers: Perry Lee Botone, Jr., Mike Gawhega, Jim Grant, Wesley J. Hudson, James Kemble, Garland Kent, Jr., Gregory Lieb, Kinsel Lieb, Stephen Little Cook, John E. Mcintosh, Patrick T. Moore, Jade Roubedeaux
Recorded at: Red Rock, Oklahoma, October 4, 1995 Format: Cassette

Southwest Pow Wow Groups

Hopi Sunshield Singers
Pow-Wow Songs Live!
CANYON RECORDS CR-6180, Recorded: Live, Format: Cassette

Various Artists
Navajo Round Dance
INDIAN HOUSE 1504
Contents: 50 Navajo round dance songs
Singers: Boniface Bonnie, Autisdy Smith, Ben J. Johnson, Donald Deal, Stella
Bonnie, Winnie Bonnie, Nellie Curley, Mary Deal
Recorded at: Klagetoh, Arizona, February 25, 1968
Tribe: Navajo
Format: Cassette, LP

Round Dance Songs Of Taos Pueblo - Volume One
INDIAN HOUSE 1001
Contents: 16 Taos round dance songs
Singers: John C. Gomez, Orlando Lujan, Ralph Lujan, Bennie Mondragon,
Ruben Romero, Louis Sandoval
Recorded at: Taos Pueblo, New Mexico, November 12, 1966
Tribe: Taos Pueblo
Format: Cassette, LP

Round Dance Songs Of Taos Pueblo - Volume Two
INDIAN HOUSE 1002
Contents: 15 Taos round dance songs
Singers: John C. Gomez, Orlando Lujan, Ralph Lujan, Bennie Mondragon,
Ruben Romero, Louis Sandoval
Recorded at: Taos Pueblo, New Mexico, November 12, 1966-- Continued from
INDIAN HOUSE 1001
Tribe: Taos Pueblo
Format: Cassette, LP

Taos Pueblo Round Dance
INDIAN HOUSE 1005
Contents: 13 Taos round dance songs
Singers: Jimmy Cordova, Orlando Lujan, Ernest Martinez, Ruben Romero
Recorded at: Taos Pueblo, New Mexico, April 22, 1974
Tribe: Taos Pueblo
Format:Cassette

Taos Pueblo Round Dance Songs - Volume 1
INDIAN HOUSE 1006
Contents: 15 Taos round dance songs
Singers: Joe Luis Mirabal, John A. Mirabal, John C. Romero, Manuel Sandy,
Jerry G. Lujan
Recorded at: Taos Pueblo, New Mexico, May 31, 1987
Tribe: Taos Pueblo
Format: Cassette

72

Taos Pueblo Round Dance Songs - Volume 2
INDIAN HOUSE 1007
Contents: 16 Taos round dance songs
Singers: Joe Luis Mirabal, John A. Mirabal, John C. Romero, Manuel Sandy, Jerry G. Lujan
Recorded at: Taos Pueblo, New Mexico, May 31, 1987-- Continued from INDIAN HOUSE 1006
Tribe: Taos Pueblo
Format: Cassette

Taos Pueblo Tribal Songs
INDIAN HOUSE RECORDS SC 205
Contents:10 round dance songs, 2 war dance songs
Singers: Joe Trinidad Archuleta, George Archuleta, Joe Suazo
Recorded: Taos Pueblo, NM, July 27, 1953.
Tribe:Taos Pueblo
Format: Cassette

Taos Round Dance - Part 1
INDIAN HOUSE 1003
Contents: 16 Taos round dance songs
Singers: Steven Archuleta, Andy Lujan, Frederick Lujan, Jr., Hubert Lujan, Joseph Luis Mirabal, John C. Romero, Manuel Sandy
Recorded at: Taos Pueblo, New Mexico, August 11, 1969
Tribe: Taos Pueblo
Format: Cassette

Taos Round Dance - Part 2
INDIAN HOUSE 1004
Contents: 16 Taos round dance songs
Singers: Steven Archuleta, Andy Lujan, Frederick Lujan, Jr., Hubert Lujan, Joseph Luis Mirabal, John C. Romero, Manuel Sandy
Recorded at: Taos Pueblo, New Mexico, August 11, 1969-- Continued from INDIAN HOUSE 1003
Tribe: Taos Pueblo
Format: Cassette, LP

Traditional Music

Apache Music

Cassa, Murphy
Vol. 1, Remembering Murphy Cassa
CANYON RECORDS CR-703, Tribe: Apache, Recorded: Studio, Format: Cassette

Vol. 2, Remembering Murphy Cassa
CANYON RECORDS CR-704, Tribe: Apache, Recorded: Studio, Format: Cassette

Cassadore, Patsy
I Build the Wickiup
CANYON RECORDS CR-6102, Tribe: Apache, Recorded: Studio, Format: Cassette

Cassadore, Philip
Apache
CANYON RECORDS CR-6053, Tribe: Apache, Recorded: Studio, Format: Cassette

Riley & Endfield
Songs of the Arizona Apache
CANYON RECORDS CR-705, Tribe: Apache, Recorded: Studio, Format: Cassette

Various Artists
American Indian Dances
Smithsonian / Folkways 6510, Recorded: Live, Format: Cassette

Music of the Plains Apache
Smithsonian / Folkways 4252, Recorded: Live, Format: Cassette

Songs of the White Mountain Apache
CANYON RECORDS CR-6165, Tribe: Apache, Recorded: Studio, Format: Cassette

Arapaho Music

Wind River Singers
Songs of the Arapaho Sun Dance
CANYON RECORDS CR-6080, Tribe: Arapaho, Recorded: Studio, Format: Cassette

Aztec Music

Xavier Quijas Yxayotl
Aztec Dances
CANYON RECORDS CR-7045, Tribe: Aztec, Recorded: Studio, Format: Cassette

Singing Earth
CANYON RECORDS CR-7044, Tribe: Aztec, Recorded: Studio, Format: Cassette

Blackfeet Music

Big Spring & Runner
Blackfeet Hand Game Songs
CANYON RECORDS CR-6188, Tribe: Blackfeet, Recorded: Studio, Format: Cassette

Blackfoot Music

Various Artists
An Historical Album of Blackfoot Indian Music
Smithsonian / Folkways 34001, Recorded: Live, Format: Cassette

Caddo Music

Various Artists
Vol.1, Songs of the Caddo
CANYON RECORDS CR-6146, Tribe: Caddo, Recorded: Studio, Format: Cassette

Vol.2, Songs of the Caddo
CANYON RECORDS CR-6147, Tribe: Caddo, Recorded: Studio, Format: Cassette

Chemewa Music

Chemawa Singers
Chemawa Indian School Singers
CANYON RECORDS CR-6121, Tribe: Chemawa, Recorded: Studio, Format: Cassette

Intertribal Pow-Wow Songs
CANYON RECORDS CR-6196, Tribe: Chemawa, Recorded: Studio, Format: Cassette

Cheyenne Music

Various Artists
Northern Cheyenne Sun Dance Songs and Crow Tribal Sun Dance Songs
INDIAN HOUSE RECORDS SC 700
Contents: 7 Northern Cheyenne sun dance songs, 7 Crow sun dance songs
Singers: Phil Whiteman, Thomas Wooden Leg, Harvey Whiteman, J. White Dirt, Pete Whiteman, Milton Yellow Mule, Mrs. Yellow Mule
Tribe: Northern Cheyenne, Crow, Format: Cassette

Chippewa Music

The Chippewa Singers
Songs of the Chippewa
CANYON RECORDS CR-8013, Tribe: Chippewa, Recorded: Studio, Format: Cassette

Ponemah Singers
Chippewa War Dance Songs
CANYON RECORDS CR-6082, Tribe: Chippewa, Recorded: Studio, Format: Cassette

Various Artists
Plains Chippewa: Metis Music from Turtle Mountain
Smithsonian / Folkways 40411, Recorded: Live, Format: Cassette

Songs of the Chippewa Vol. 1: Minnesota Chippewa Game and Social Dance Songs
Smithsonian / Folkways 4392, Recorded: Live, Format: Cassette

Comanche Music

Mauchahty-Ware, Tom
Flute Songs of the Kiowa and Comanche
INDIAN HOUSE RECORDS IH 2512
Contents: 13 traditional songs (including the Kiowa flag song, love songs, and Comanche hymns)
Singers: Tom Mauchahty-Ware
Recorded at: Hog Creek, Oklahoma, June 1, 1978
Tribe: Kiowa, Comanche
Format: CD, Cassette
Additional information: Tom Mauchahty-Ware has been playing flute for over 20 years. Of Kiowa and Comanche descent, Tom was raised in a traditional family, and is both a skilled dancer and traditional singer. Because of his experience as a singer, his flute renditions of traditional songs are extremely accurate, so that one can almost sing along with the flute version. On this recording, Tom uses several different flutes to perform both traditional and original compositions. Extensive notes by Mauchahty-Ware explain the history of the Kiowa flute and the background of each song on the album.

Nevaquaya, Doc "Tate"
Comanche Flute Music
Smithsonian / Folkways 4328, Recorded: Studio, Format: Cassette

Cree Music

Various Artists
Music of the Algonkians Woodlands Indians: Cree, Montagnais, Naska
Smithsonian / Folkways 4253, Recorded: Live, Format: Cassette

Wood Brothers
Cree Stick Game Songs
CANYON RECORDS CR-16228, Tribe: Cree, Recorded: Studio, Format:
Cassette

Wood, Randy
Round Dance the Night Away
CANYON RECORDS (No Number), Tribe: Cree, Recorded: Studio, Format:
Cassette

Eskimo Music

Various Artists
Eskimo Songs from Alaska
Smithsonian / Folkways 4069, Recorded: Live, Format: Cassette

The Eskimos of Hudson Bay and Alaska
Smithsonian / Folkways 4444, Recorded: Live, Format: Cassette

Flathead Music

Antiste, Mary
Flathead Stick Games
CANYON RECORDS CR-8017, Tribe: Flathead, Recorded: Studio, Format:
Cassette

Various Artists
Flathead Stick Games
CANYON RECORDS CR-6105, Tribe: Flathead, Recorded: Studio, Format:
Cassette

Songs and Dances of the Flathead Indians
Smithsonian / Folkways 4445, Recorded: Live, Format: Cassette

Haida Music

Various Artists
Haida: Indian Music of the Pacific Northwest
Smithsonian / Folkways 4119, Recorded: Live, Format: Cassette

Hidatsa Music

Mandaree Singers
Vol.1, Mandan-Hidatsa Songs
CANYON RECORDS CR-6114, Recorded: Studio, Format: Cassette

Hopi Music

Numkena, Wil
Hopi Son
SOAR 147, Recorded: Studio, Format: CD, Cassette

Setima, Ben
Hopi Butterfly
CANYON RECORDS CR-6072, Tribe: Hopi, Recorded: Studio, Format: Cassette

Vol.1, Hopi Social Dance Songs
CANYON RECORDS CR-6107, Tribe: Hopi, Recorded: Studio, Format: Cassette

Vol.2, Hopi Social Dance Songs
CANYON RECORDS CR-6108, Tribe: Hopi, Recorded: Studio, Format: Cassette

Various Artists
Hopi Katcina Songs and Six Songs by Hopi Chanters
Smithsonian / Folkways 4394, Recorded: Live, Format: Cassette

Sounds Of Indian America - Plains and Southwest
INDIAN HOUSE RECORDS IH 9501
Contents: Hopi Buffalo Dance, Jemez Eagle Dance, Ute Bear Dance, San Juan
Butterfly Dance, Zuni Rain Song by the Olla Maidens, Navajo Feather Dance,
Taos Belt Dance, Pawnee Ghost Dance, Zuni Doll Dance, Ouechan Night Hawk
Dance, Crow Sun Dance, San Carlos Apache Crown Dance, Laguna Turkey
Dance, Kiowa Attack Dance
Recorded live at: the 48th Inter-Tribal Indian Ceremonial, Gallup, New Mexico,
August 14-17, 1969
Tribes: Hopi Pueblo, Jemez Pueblo, Ute, San Juan Pueblo, Zuni Pueblo, Navajo,
Taos Pueblo, Pawnee, Zuni Pueblo, Quechan, Crow, San Carlos Apache,
Laguna Pueblo, Kiowa
Format: CD, Cassette
Additional information: In response to requests for an introduction to American
Indian music, this recording presents a wide range of songs from many different
tribes, including Pueblo, Navajo, Apache, Southern Plains, Northern Plains,
Plateau, and California singing groups

Pueblo Songs Of The Southwest
INDIAN HOUSE RECORDS IH 9502
Contents: Hopi Basket Dance, Hopi Butterfly Dance, Jemez Buffalo Dance, San
Juan Basket Dance, Zuni Rainbow Dance, Laguna Arrow Dance, Laguna Eagle
Dance, Laguna Buffalo Dance
Recorded live at: the 48th Inter-Tribal Indian Ceremonial, Gallup, New Mexico,
August 14-17, 1969
Tribes: Hopi Pueblo, Jemez Pueblo, San Juan Pueblo, Zuni Pueblo, Laguna
Pueblo
Format: Cassette

Hualapai Music

Mahone, Keith
> *Bird Songs of the Hualapai*
> CANYON RECORDS CR-6280, Tribe: Hualapai, Recorded: Studio, Format: Cassette

Intertribal Music

Bala Sinem Choir
> *Vol.1, American Indian Songs*
> CANYON RECORDS CR-6110, Recorded: Studio, Format: Cassette
>
> *Vol.2, Walk in Beauty, My Children*
> CANYON RECORDS CR-6149, Recorded: Studio, Format: Cassette

Cody, Robert Tree
> *Dreams from the Grandfather*
> CANYON RECORDS CR-554, Recorded: Studio, Format: Cassette
>
> *Lullabies & Other Flute Songs*
> CANYON RECORDS CR-552, Recorded: Studio, Format: Cassette
>
> *Traditional Flute Music*
> CANYON RECORDS CR-551, Recorded: Studio, Format: Cassette
>
> *Young Eagle's Flight*
> CANYON RECORDS CR-553, Recorded: Studio, Format: Cassette

Edwards, Hovia
> *Morning Star*
> CANYON RECORDS CR-557, Recorded: Studio, Format: Cassette

The Boyz
> *Down 4 Life*
> CANYON RECORDS CR-6334, Recorded: Studio, Format: Cassette

Tha Tribe
> *Live from Tornado Alley!*
> CANYON RECORDS CR-6326, Recorded: Studio, Format: Cassette
>
> *T2K*
> CANYON RECORDS CR-6320, Recorded: Studio, Format: Cassette
>
> *'N Action*
> CANYON RECORDS CR-6340, Recorded: Studio, Format: Cassette
>
> *Winter Storm*
> CANYON RECORDS CR-6351, Recorded: Studio, Format: Cassette

Thunderbird Sisters
Contemporary American Indian Songs
Smithsonian / Folkways 37255, Recorded: Studio, Format: Cassette

Various Artists
Creations Journey: Native American Music
Smithsonian Folkways 40410, Recorded: Studio, Format: CD, Cassette
Notes: Presented by the National Museum of the American Indian. From
powwow music to Christian songs in Cherokee to Irish reels, Native peoples from
the U.S., Canada, Mexico, and Bolivia present living traditions and crossovers to
Euro-American musics. Recorded in New York City and Washington d.c., in 1992
and 1993. Package includes detailed notes in a beautifully illustrated booklet.

Cry from the Earth: Music of the North American Indians
Smithsonian / Folkways 37777, Recorded: Studio, Format: Cassette

Great Plains Singers & Songs
CANYON RECORDS CR-6052, Recorded: Studio, Format: Cassette

Healing Songs of the American Indians
Smithsonian / Folkways 4251, Recorded: Live, Format: Cassette

Heartbeat: Voices of First Nations Women
Smithsonian Folkways 40415, Recorded: Studio, Format: CD, Cassette
Notes: Powerful living music from Native women in the United States and
Canada includes performances rarely heard beyond these artists' communities.
Ceremonial and social songs traditionally sung by women, other music now
performed by women, and material that combines traditional and contemporary
themes and musical forms. 34 selections present a seamless range of solo,
choral, and instrumental pieces, forming pulsating and driving music, the heart of
Indian Country.

Heartbeat 2: More Voices of First Nations Women
Smithsonian Folkways 40455, Recorded: Studio, Format: CD
Notes:The Highly acclaimed 1995 Smithsonian Folkways release,
Heartbeat: Voices of First Nations Women, introduced the public to a
rare and dynamic but little-known Native American music. *Heartbeat 2*
includes social and ceremonial dance songs, war, honor, and story
songs from Native North America, as well as music in contemporary
styles, including flute songs, poetry set jazz, and pop-oriented folk song.

Indian Music of the Canadian Plains
Smithsonian / Folkways 4464, Recorded: Live, Format: Cassette

Indian Music of the Southwest
Smithsonian / Folkways 8850, Recorded: Live, Format: Cassette

Music of New Mexico: Native American Traditions
Smithsonian Folkways 40408, Recorded: Studio, Format: CD, Cassette
Notes:This portrait of Pueblo, Navajo, and Mescalero Apache music from New Mexico (recorded in 1992) reveals a remarkable breadth of Native American song, from a traditional San Juan Pueblo Cloud Dance song to modern Navajo songs. 68 minutes. Produced by Howard Bass. Annotated by Edward Wapp Wahpeconiah.

Music of the American Indians of the Southwest
Smithsonian / Folkways 4420, Recorded: Live, Format: Cassette

Navajo Songs
Smithsonian Folkways 40403, Recorded: Studio, Format: CD, Cassette
Notes: The lifestyles, philosophies, and traditions of the Navajo nation are represented by songs for herding, planting, harvesting, hunting, blessing hogans, and soothing children. The 1933 and 1940 field recordings from settlements in New Mexico and Arizona beautifully document a music largely vocal and highly melodic with relatively short song phrases repeated, divided, and combined in intriguingly complex ways. Recorded by Laura Boulton. Compiled and annotated by David McAllester and Charlotte Frisbie.

Plains Chippewa: Metis Music from Turtle Mountain
Smithsonian Folkways 40411, Recorded: Studio, Format: CD, Cassette
Notes: From traditional drum songs to French children's songs, and from Scottish fiddle dance tunes to contemporary country and rock 'n' roll, this recording presents music heard today on the Turtle Mountain Reservation which straddles the border between the U.S. and Canada. A passionate and lively portrait of the history and daily lives of an indigenous American culture born by the contact of American Indians with Europeans. Compiled and annotated by Nicholas Curchin Peterson Vrooman.

Songs of the Great Lakes Indians
Smithsonian / Folkways 4003, Recorded: Live, Format: Cassette

Sounds of the American Southwest
Smithsonian / Folkways 6122, Recorded: Live, Format: Cassette

The Song of the Indian
CANYON RECORDS CR-6050, Recorded: Studio, Format: Cassette

Traditional Voices
CANYON RECORDS CR-7053, Recorded: Studio, Format: Cassette

Vol. 1, Voices Across the Canyon
CANYON RECORDS CR-7051, Recorded: Studio, Format: Cassette

Vol. 2, Voices Across the Canyon
CANYON RECORDS CR-7052, Recorded: Studio, Format: Cassette

Vol. 3, Voices Across the Canyon
CANYON RECORDS CR-7054, Recorded: Studio, Format: Cassette

Vol. 4, Voices Across the Canyon
CANYON RECORDS CR-7055, Recorded: Studio, Format: Cassette

Vol. 5, Voices Across the Canyon
CANYON RECORDS CR-7056, Recorded: Studio, Format: Cassette

Wood That Sings: Indian Fiddle Music of the Americas
Smithsonian Folkways 40472, Recorded: Studio, Format: CD, Cassette
Notes: This anthology of Indian fiddle music of the Americas features
performances by Indian musicians from Nova Scotia and Manitoba to North
Dakota and Arizona, to Mexico, Peru, and elsewhere in Latin America. Using this
most popular of instruments as a way to explore the great variety and creativity of
Indian musical traditions—from chicken scratch to the indigenous Apache
fiddle—this recording expresses the capacity of Native cultures to adapt and
synthesize non-Native influences.

Young Bird
Change for Life
CANYON RECORDS CR-6341, Recorded: Studio, Format: Cassette

Deja Vu
CANYON RECORDS CR-6289, Recorded: Studio, Format: Cassette

Double Platinum
CANYON RECORDS CR-6347, Recorded: Studio, Format: Cassette

Down 4 Life
CANYON RECORDS CR-6334, Recorded: Studio, Format: Cassette

Only the Strong Survive
CANYON RECORDS CR-6354, Recorded: Studio, Format: Cassette

Rendezvous
CANYON RECORDS CR-6319, Recorded: Studio, Format: Cassette

Southern and Northern Style Pow-Wow Songs
CANYON RECORDS CR-6361, Recorded: Studio, Format: Cassette

Word Up!
CANYON RECORDS CR-6329, Recorded: Studio, Format: Cassette

Kiowa Music

Bad Medicine Singers
Vol.1, Southern Pow-Wow Songs Live
CANYON RECORDS CR-6251, Tribe: Kiowa, Recorded: Studio, Format:
Cassette

Vol.2, "Dance Your Style"
CANYON RECORDS CR-6252, Tribe: Kiowa, Recorded: Studio, Format:
Cassette

Brave Scout Singers
Brave Scout Singers
CANYON RECORDS CR-6172, Tribe: Kiowa, Recorded: Studio, Format: Cassette

Fort Oakland Ramblers
When He Paints His Face
CANYON RECORDS CR-6281, Tribe: Kiowa, Recorded: Studio, Format: Cassette

Kaulaity & Kozad
Kiowa Black Leggings Society Songs
CANYON RECORDS CR-6167, Tribe: Kiowa, Recorded: Studio, Format: Cassette

Kiowa Dance Group Singers
Kiowa Scalp & Victory Dance Songs
CANYON RECORDS CR-6166 Tribe: Kiowa, Recorded: Studio, Format: Cassette

Gourd Dance Songs of the Kiowa
CANYON RECORDS CR-6148 Tribe: Kiowa, Recorded: Studio, Format: Cassette

Koomsa Tribal Singers
Kiowa!
CANYON RECORDS CR-6145, Tribe: Kiowa, Recorded: Studio, Format: Cassette

Mauchahty-Ware, Tom
Flute Songs of the Kiowa and Comanche
INDIAN HOUSE RECORDS IH 2512
Contents: 13 traditional songs (including the Kiowa flag song, love songs, and Comanche hymns)
Singers: Tom Mauchahty-Ware
Recorded at: Hog Creek, Oklahoma, June 1, 1978
Tribe: Kiowa, Comanche
Format: CD, Cassette
Additional information: Tom Mauchahty-Ware has been playing flute for over 20 years. Of Kiowa and Comanche descent, Tom was raised in a traditional family, and is both a skilled dancer and traditional singer. Because of his experience as a singer, his flute renditions of traditional songs are extremely accurate, so that one can almost sing along with the flute version. On this recording, Tom uses several different flutes to perform both traditional and original compositions. Extensive notes by Mauchahty-Ware explain the history of the Kiowa flute and the background of each song on the album.

Various Artists

Handgame of the Kiowa, Kiowa Apache and Comanche - Volume 1: Carnegie Roadrunners vs. Billy Goat Hill
INDIAN HOUSE RECORDS IH 2501
Contents: 23 handgame songs
Singers: Carnegie Roadrunners, Billy Goat Hill
Recorded live at: Carnegie, Oklahoma, November 24, 1968
Tribe: Kiowa, Kiowa-Apache, Comanche
Format: Cassette

Handgame of the Kiowa, Kiowa Apache and Comanche - Volume 2: Carnegie Roadrunners vs. Billy Goat Hill
INDIAN HOUSE RECORDS IH 2502 Contents: 23 handgame songs
Singers: Carnegie Roadrunners, Billy Goat Hill
Recorded live at: Carnegie, Oklahoma, November 24, 1968-- Continued from
INDIAN HOUSE IH 2501
Tribe: Kiowa, Kiowa-Apache, Comanche
Format: Cassette, LP

Kiowa
Smithsonian / Folkways 4393, Recorded: Live, Format: Cassette

Kiowa Black-Leg Warriors Society Songs
INDIAN HOUSE RECORDS SC 305
Contents: 12 Kiowa Black-Leg Society songs
Singers: Leonard Cozad, Jasper Sankadota, OINDIAN HOUSE SCar Tahlo,
Laura Tahlo
Recorded at: Carnegie, Oklahoma, January 22, 1964
Tribe: Kiowa
Format: Cassette

Kiowa Church Songs - Volume 1
INDIAN HOUSE RECORDS IH 2506
Contents: 22 Kiowa Christian church songs
Singers: David Apekaum, Ray Cozad, Harry Domebo, Walter Geionety, Tom
Tointigh, Ruby Beaver, Kathleen Redbone, Joyce Robinson, Nancy Tointigh
Recorded at: Carnegie, Oklahoma, March 31, 1971
Tribe: Kiowa
Format: Cassette

Kiowa Church Songs - Volume 2
INDIAN HOUSE RECORDS IH 2507
Contents: 18 Kiowa Christian church songs
Singers: David Apekaum, Ray Cozad, Harry Domebo, Walter Geionety, Tom
Tointigh, Ruby Beaver, Kathleen Redbone, Joyce Robinson, Nancy Tointigh
Recorded at: Carnegie, Oklahoma, March 31, 1971--Continued from INDIAN
HOUSE IH 2506
Tribe: Kiowa
Format: Cassette, LP

Kiowa Circle & Two-Step Songs
INDIAN HOUSE RECORDS SC 278
Contents: 12 round dance songs
Singers: Leonard Cozad, Jasper Sankadota, OINDIAN HOUSE SCar Tahlo,
Laura Tahlo Recorded at: Carnegie, Oklahoma, January 22, 1964 Tribe: Kiowa

Kiowa Gourd Dance - Volume 1
INDIAN HOUSE RECORDS IH 2503
Contents: 12 Kiowa gourd dance songs
Singers: Daniel Cozad, Joe Cozad, Larry Cozad, Leonard Cozad Sr., Billy
Hunting Horse, Adam Kaulaity, Vincent Spotted Bird, Yale Spotted Bird, Velma
Cozad, Barbara Ahhaitty Monoessy, Dobbin Monoessy, Naomi Svitak Dancers
are David Apekaum, Marty Autaubo, Richard Kauahquo, Elrod Monoessy, Curtis
Tointigh
Recorded at: Carnegie, Oklahoma, June 10, 1974
Tribe: Kiowa
Format: CD, Cassette

Kiowa Gourd Dance - Volume 2
INDIAN HOUSE RECORDS IH 2504
Contents: 11 Kiowa gourd dance songs
Singers: Daniel Cozad, Joe Cozad, Larry Cozad, Leonard Cozad Sr., Billy
Hunting Horse, Adam Kaulaity, Vincent Spotted Bird, Yale Spotted Bird, Velma
Cozad, Barbara Ahhaitty Monoessy, Dobbin Monoessy, Naomi Svitak Dancers
are David Apekaum, Marty Autaubo, Richard Kauahquo, Elrod Monoessy, Curtis
Tointigh
Recorded at: Carnegie, Oklahoma, June 10, 1974--Continued from INDIAN
HOUSE IH 2503
Tribe: Kiowa
Format: Cassette

Kiowa Gourd Dance Songs
CANYON RECORDS CR-6103, Tribe: Kiowa, Recorded: Studio, Format:
Cassette

Kiowa "49" & Round Dance Songs
CANYON RECORDS CR-6087, Tribe: Kiowa, Recorded: Studio, Format:
Cassette

Kiowa 49 - War Expedition Songs
INDIAN HOUSE RECORDS IH 2505
Contents: 17 Kiowa "49" songs
Singers: Gregory Haumpy, Billy Hunting Horse, Ralph Kotay, Bill Koomsa Jr.,
Barbara Ahhaitty, Pearl Kerche, Angeline Koomsa, Nan B. Koomsa, Wilda
Koomsa
Recorded at: Carnegie, Oklahoma, April 29, 1969
Tribe: Kiowa
Format: Cassette, LP

Kiowa Warriors Dance Songs and War Expedition ("49") Songs
INDIAN HOUSE RECORDS SC 131
Contents: 8 Kiowa warriors dance songs, 7 Kiowa war expedition ("49") songs
Singers: "The Soundchief Singers": James Aunguoe, Nathan Doyebi, Ernest Red Bird, Ruth Red Bird
Tribe: Kiowa
Format: Cassette

Songs Of The O-Ho-Mah Lodge - Kiowa War Dance Society - Volume 1
INDIAN HOUSE RECORDS IH 2510
Contents: 15 traditional O-Ho-Mah individual songs
Singers: Parker Emhoolah, Ralph Kotay, Bill Ware, Mac Whitehorse, Roland Whitehorse, Florene Whitehorse Taylor
Recorded at: Stecker, Oklahoma, October 25, 1994
Tribe: Kiowa
Format: Cassette

Songs Of The O-Ho-Mah Lodge - Kiowa War Dance Society - Volume 2
INDIAN HOUSE RECORDS IH 2511
Contents: 11 traditional O-Ho-Mah individual songs
Singers: Parker Emhoolah, Ralph Kotay, Bill Ware, Mac Whitehorse, Roland Whitehorse, Florene Whitehorse Taylor
Recorded at: Stecker, Oklahoma, October 25, 1994--Continued from INDIAN HOUSE IH 2510
Tribe: Kiowa
Format: Cassette

Kutchin Music

Various Artists
Music of the Kutchin Indians of Alaska
Smithsonian / Folkways 4070, Recorded: Live, Format: Cassette

Kwakiutl Music

Various Artists
Kwakitul: Indian Music of the Pacific Northwest
Smithsonian / Folkways 4122, Recorded: Live, Format: Cassette

Laguna Music

Setima, Ben
Songs from Laguna
CANYON RECORDS CR-6058, Tribe: Laguna, Recorded: Studio, Format: Cassette

Mesquakie Music

Mesquakie Bear Singers
Mesquakie War Dance Songs
CANYON RECORDS CR-6090, Tribe: Mesquakie, Recorded: Studio, Format:
Cassette

Woodland Singers
Traditional Mesquakie Songs
CANYON RECORDS CR-6194, Tribe: Mesquakie, Recorded: Studio, Format:
Cassette

Navajo Music

Begaye, Jay
The Beauty Way
CANYON RECORDS CR-6282, Tribe: Navajo, Recorded: Studio, Format:
Cassette

The Long Walk: Hwééldi
CANYON RECORDS CR-628, Tribe: Navajo, Recorded: Studio, Format:
Cassette

Round Dance in Beauty
CANYON RECORDS CR-6328, Tribe: Navajo, Recorded: Studio, Format:
Cassette

Bennett, Kay
Kaibah - Navajo Love Songs
CANYON RECORDS CR-7167, Tribe: Navajo, Recorded: Studio, Format:
Cassette

Bilagody, James
Beauty Ways
SOAR 132, Recorded: Studio, Format: CD, Cassette

Bita Hochee Travelers
Midnight Sweetheart
CANYON RECORDS CR-6168, Tribe: Navajo, Recorded: Studio, Format:
Cassette

Bodoway Western Trail
Two-Step & Skip Dance Songs
CANYON RECORDS CR-7165, Tribe: Navajo, Recorded: Studio, Format:
Cassette

Chinle Swin' Echoes
Making Memories
SOAR 110, Recorded: Studio, Format: Cassette

Voices from Canyon de Chelly
SOAR 130, Recorded: Studio, Format: Cassette

Chinle Valley Boys
Vol.3, Two-Step & Skip Dance Songs
CANYON RECORDS CR-7141, Tribe: Navajo, Recorded: Studio, Format: Cassette

Vol.4, Two-Step & Skip Dance Songs
CANYON RECORDS CR-7142, Tribe: Navajo, Recorded: Studio, Format: Cassette

Chinle Valley Singers
Vol.1, Two-Step & Skip Dance Songs
CANYON RECORDS CR-7134, Tribe: Navajo, Recorded: Studio, Format: Cassette

Vol.2, Songs of the Old Time
CANYON RECORDS CR-7135, Tribe: Navajo, Recorded: Studio, Format: Cassette

Vol.3, Family Traditional Songs
CANYON RECORDS CR-7171, Tribe: Navajo, Recorded: Studio, Format: Cassette

Dennehotso Swinging Wranglers
Vol.4, 14 Karat Mind
CANYON RECORDS CR-7136, Tribe: Navajo, Recorded: Studio, Format: Cassette

Four Corners Singers
Vol.1, Squaw Dance Songs
CANYON RECORDS CR-8044, Tribe: Navajo, Recorded: Studio, Format: Cassette

Vol.2, Skip Dance Songs
CANYON RECORDS CR-8045, Tribe: Navajo, Recorded: Studio, Format: Cassette

Vol.3, Two-Step Dance Songs
CANYON RECORDS CR-8048, Tribe: Navajo, Recorded: Studio, Format: Cassette

Vol.4, Skip & Two-Step Dance Songs
CANYON RECORDS CR-8049, Tribe: Navajo, Recorded: Studio, Format: Cassette

Vol.5, Two-Step & Skip Dance Songs
CANYON RECORDS CR-7143, Tribe: Navajo, Recorded: Studio, Format: Cassette

Vol.6, Two-Step & Skip Dance Songs
CANYON RECORDS CR-7144, Tribe: Navajo, Recorded: Studio, Format: Cassette

Four Corners Yei Be Chai
Yei Be Chai Songs
CANYON RECORDS CR-7152, Tribe: Navajo, Recorded: Studio, Format: Cassette

Jones Benally
Navajo Reflections
CANYON RECORDS CR-16275, Tribe: Navajo, Recorded: Studio, Format: Cassette

Klagetoh Maiden Singers
Klagetoh Maiden Singers
INDIAN HOUSE RECORDS IH 1508
Contents: 4 Navajo spin dance songs, 5 walking dance songs, 5 round dance songs, 10 two-step songs
Singers: Joycetta Bonnie, Rose M. Bonnie, Winnie Bonnie, Marie E. Brown, Bertha Johnson
Recorded at: Klagetoh, Arizona, April 21, 1974
Tribe: Navajo
Format: Cassette

The Klagetoh Swingers
Navajo Songs About Love - Volume 1: The Klagetoh Swingers
INDIAN HOUSE RECORDS IH 1509
Contents: 13 contemporary-style Navajo dance songs (from the Enemy Way Ceremony)
Singers: Amos Y. Begay, Frank J. Begay, Ted B. Bonnie, Ned T. Clark, Ben J. Johnson, Joe J. Roanhorse
Recorded at: Klagetoh, Arizona, November 17, 1974
Tribe: Navajo
Format: Cassette, LP

Navajo Songs About Love - Volume 2: The Klagetoh Swingers
INDIAN HOUSE RECORDS IH 1510
Contents: 13 contemporary-style Navajo dance songs (from the Enemy Way Ceremony)
Singers: Amos Y. Begay, Frank J. Begay, Ted B. Bonnie, Ned T. Clark, Ben J. Johnson, Joe J. Roanhorse--Continued from IH 1509
Recorded at: Klagetoh, Arizona, November 17, 1974
Tribe: Navajo
Format: Cassette, LP

Navajo Songs About Love - Volume 3: The Klagetoh Swingers
INDIAN HOUSE RECORDS IH 1511
Contents:15 contemporary-style Navajo dance songs
Singers: Frank J. Begay, Ted B. Bonnie, Ned T. Clark, Robert P. Roan
Recorded at: Klagetoh, Arizona, Nov. 13, 1977
Tribe: Navajo Format: Cassette, LP

Navajo Songs About Love - Volume 4: The Klagetoh Swingers
INDIAN HOUSE RECORDS IH 1512
Contents: 9 contemporary-style Navajo two-step songs
Singers: Frank J. Begay, Ted B. Bonnie, Ned T. Clark, Robert P. Roan--
Continued from IH 1511
Recorded at: Recorded at Klagetoh, Arizona, Nov. 13, 1977
Tribe: Navajo
Format: Cassette, LP

The Klagetoh Swingers - Navajo Love Songs: Volume 5
INDIAN HOUSE RECORDS IH 1513
Contents: 2 spin dance songs & 18 skip dance songs
Singers: Ted B. Bonnie, Ned Tsosie Clark, Frank J. Begay, Robert P. Roan,
Arthur P. Roan, Bennie Silversmith, Johnny Dealison
Recorded at: Klagetoh, Arizona, July 30, 1980
Tribe: Navajo
Format: Cassette

The Klagetoh Swingers - Navajo Love Songs: Volume 6
INDIAN HOUSE RECORDS IH 1514
Contents: 11 two-step songs
Singers: Ted B. Bonnie, Ned Tsosie Clark, Frank J. Begay, Robert P. Roan,
Arthur P. Roan, Bennie Silversmith, Johnny Dealison--Continued From IH 1513
Recorded at: Klagetoh, Arizona
Tribe: Navajo
Format: Cassette

Mitchell, Davis
A Good year for the Rose
SOAR 121, Recorded: Studio, Format: CD, Cassette

The Navaho Kid Rides Again
SOAR 112, Recorded: Studio, Format: CD, Cassette

Navajo Singer Sings for You
SOAR 107, Recorded: Studio, Format: CD, Cassette

Songs from a Distant Drum
SOAR 137, Recorded: Studio, Format: Cassette

Monument Valley Singers
Traditional Navajo Songs
CANYON RECORDS CR-7178, Tribe: Navajo, Recorded: Studio, Format:
Cassette

For Japanese Girls
CANYON RECORDS CR-7180, Tribe: Navajo, Recorded: Studio, Format:
Cassette

Nanaba, Midge
Traditional Navajo Songs
CANYON RECORDS CR-7146, Tribe: Navajo, Recorded: Studio, Format: Cassette

Natay, Ed Lee
Memories of Navajoland
CANYON RECORDS CR-6057, Tribe: Navajo, Recorded: Studio, Format: Cassette

Natay, Navajo Singer
CANYON RECORDS CR-6160
Contents: Contains all of CR-6057 as bonus material.
Tribe: Navajo
Format: Compact disc

Navajo Nation Singers
Traditional Love Songs
CANYON RECORDS CR-7174, Tribe: Navajo, Recorded: Studio, Format: Cassette

Navajo Nation Swingers
Navajo Style
SOAR 123, Recorded: Studio, Format: Cassette

Nez, D. J.
My Heroes Have Always Been Indians
SOAR 111, Recorded: Studio, Format: Cassette

Navajo in Paris
SOAR 128, Recorded: Studio, Format: Cassette

Northern Ranchers
Two Step & Skip Dance Songs
CANYON RECORDS CR-7173, Tribe: Navajo, Recorded: Studio, Format: Cassette

Radmilla, Cody
Seed of Life
CANYON RECORDS CR-6345, Tribe: Navajo, Recorded: Studio, Format: Cassette

Rock Point Singers
Navajo Skip Dance and Two-Step Songs - Volume 1: Rock Point Singers
INDIAN HOUSE RECORDS IH 1531
Contents: 7 skip dance songs, 5 two-step songs
Singers: Harry Tso Begay, Julius M. Begay, Glen Tsosie, Kenneth Woody Jr., Sam Woody
Recorded at: Rock Point, Arizona, November 22, 1981
Tribe: Navajo
Format: Cassette

Navajo Skip Dance and Two-Step Songs - Volume 2: Rock Point Singers
INDIAN HOUSE RECORDS IH 1532
Contents: 5 skip dance songs, 7 two-step songs
Singers: Harry Tso Begay, Julius M. Begay, Glen Tsosie, Kenneth Woody Jr.,
Sam Woody--Continued from IH 1531
Tribe: Navajo
Format: Cassette

Vol.3, Love Songs
CANYON RECORDS CR-7140) , Tribe: Navajo, Recorded: Studio, Format:
Cassette

Southern Maiden Singers
Southern Maiden Singers - Navajo Skip Dance & Two-Step Songs
INDIAN HOUSE RECORDS IH 1535
Contents: 6 skip dance, 6 two-step songs
Singers: Lucy Bitsilly, Mary S. Chee, Darlene Kinlecheenie, Irene Kinlecheenie,
Marlene Kinlechennie, Mary Lou Kinlecheenie
Recorded at: Greasewood, Arizona, May 19, 1984 Tribe: Navajo, Cassette

Southwestern Singers
Vol.1, Two-Step & Skip Dance Songs
CANYON RECORDS CR-7163, Tribe: Navajo, Recorded: Studio, Format:
Cassette

Vol.2, Two-Step & Skip Dance Songs
CANYON RECORDS CR-7168, Tribe: Navajo, Recorded: Studio, Format:
Cassette

Sweethearts of Navajoland
Vol.1, Traditional Two-Step Songs
CANYON RECORDS CR-7159, Tribe: Navajo, Recorded: Studio, Format:
Cassette

Vol.2, Traditional Two-Step Songs
CANYON RECORDS CR-7160, Tribe: Navajo, Recorded: Studio, Format:
Cassette

Vol.3, Exploring Europe
CANYON RECORDS CR-7161, Tribe: Navajo, Recorded: Studio, Format:
Cassette

Vol.4, Social Songs
CANYON RECORDS CR-7162, Tribe: Navajo, Recorded: Studio, Format:
Cassette

Vol.5, Social Songs
CANYON RECORDS CR-7164, Tribe: Navajo, Recorded: Studio, Format:
Cassette

Thunderbird Maidens
Young Voices of the Western Navajo
CANYON RECORDS CR-7166, Tribe: Navajo, Recorded: Studio, Format:
Cassette

Todí Neesh Zhee Singers
Dedicated to the Younger Generation
CANYON RECORDS CR-7137, Tribe: Navajo, Recorded: Studio, Format:
Cassette

For All Eternity
CANYON RECORDS CR-7179, Tribe: Navajo, Recorded: Studio, Format:
Cassette

In Beauty We Sing & Dance
CANYON RECORDS CR-7176, Tribe: Navajo, Recorded: Studio, Format:
Cassette

Sing Me That Good Ol' Song
CANYON RECORDS CR-7177, Tribe: Navajo, Recorded: Studio, Format:
Cassette

The New Beginning to an Old Tradition
CANYON RECORDS CR-7172, Tribe: Navajo, Recorded: Studio, Format:
Cassette
Through the Old Eyes, the Young Arise
CANYON RECORDS CR-7170, Tribe: Navajo, Recorded: Studio, Format:
Cassette

Tsosie Clark, Ned
King of the Navajo Songs and Dance
SOAR 108, Recorded: Studio, Format: Cassette

Tsinajinnie, Delphine
Mother's Word
CANYON RECORDS CR-6325, Tribe: Navajo, Recorded: Studio, Format:
Cassette

Tsi Yi Tohi Singers
Vol.3, Navajo Two-Step Songs
CANYON RECORDS CR-7153, Tribe: Navajo, Recorded: Studio, Format:
Cassette

Turtle Mountain Singers
Turtle Mountain Singers - Navajo Social Dance Songs
INDIAN HOUSE RECORDS IH 1523
Contents:10 social dance songs (5 two-step, 5 skip dance)
Singers: John P. Comanche, Jimmie Castillo, Samuel C. Harrison, John B.
Dennison, Kee Y. Trujillo, Ernest Chavez, Renzo Comanche, Benson Trujillo
Recorded at: Lybrook, New Mexico, March 14, 1987
Tribe: Navajo Format: Cassette

Turtle Mountain Singers - Navajo Social Dance Songs, Eastern Style
INDIAN HOUSE RECORDS IH 1524
Contents: 10 social dance songs (5 two-step, 5 skip sance)
Singers: John P. Comanche, Jimmie Castillo, Samuel C. Harrison, John B. Dennison, Kee Y. Trujillo, Ernest Chavez, Renzo Comanche, Benson Trujillo
Recorded at: Lybrook, New Mexico, March 14, 1987
Tribe: Navajo
Format: Cassette

Turtle Mountain Singers - Welcome to Navajo Land
INDIAN HOUSE RECORDS IH 1525
Contents: 10 social dance songs (5 two-step, 5 skip dance)
Singers: John P. Comanche, Jimmie Castillo, Samuel C. Harrison, Ernest Chavez, Kee Y. Trujillo, Johnny B. Dennison, Benson Trujillo
Recorded at: Lybrook, New Mexico, April 14, 1990
Tribe: Navajo
Format: Cassette

Turtle Mountain Singers - Early This Morning I Heard My Horse Calling
INDIAN HOUSE RECORDS IH 1526
Contents: 10 social dance songs (5 two-step, 5 skip dance)
Singers: John P. Comanche, Jimmie Castillo, Samuel C. Harrison, Kee Y. Trujillo
Recorded at: Taos, New Mexico, June 23, 1990
Tribe: Navajo
Format: Cassette

Various Artists
Navajo - Songs of the Diné
CANYON RECORDS CR-6055, Tribe: Navajo, Recorded: Studio, Format: Cassette

Navajo Songs
Smithsonian / Folkways SF 40403, Recorded: Studio, Format: CD, Cassette

Navajo Squaw Dance Songs
CANYON RECORDS CR-6067, Tribe: Navajo, Recorded: Studio, Format: Cassette

Traditional Navajo Songs
CANYON RECORDS CR-6064, Tribe: Navajo, Recorded: Studio, Format: Cassette

Vol.1, Two-Step Songs
CANYON RECORDS CR-7132, Tribe: Navajo, Recorded: Studio, Format: Cassette

Vol.2, Skip Songs
CANYON RECORDS CR-7133, Tribe: Navajo, Recorded: Studio, Format: Cassette

Yei-Be-Chai Songs
CANYON RECORDS CR-6069, Tribe: Navajo, Recorded: Studio, Format: Cassette

Navajo Gift Songs & Round Dance
INDIAN HOUSE RECORDS IH 1505
Contents: 21 Navajo gift songs, 29 Navajo round dance songs (from the Enemy Way Ceremony)
Singers: Boniface Bonnie, Autisdy Smith, M.D. Johnson, Roy Bonnie, Ben J. Johnson, Ted Bonnie, Benny Roanhorse, Donald Deal, Bertha Bonnie, Stella Bonnie, Winnie Bonnie, Nellie Curley, Mary Deal
Recorded at: Klagetoh, Arizona, March 16, 1968
Tribe: Navajo
Format: Cassette, LP

Navajo Corn Grinding and Shoe Game Songs
INDIAN HOUSE RECORDS IH 1507
Contents: 7 corn grinding songs, 13 shoe game songs
Singers: Boniface Bonnie, Ted B. Bonnie, Mike D. Johnson, Chester Roan, Autisdy Smith, Rose M. Bonnie, Winnie Bonnie, Marie E. Brown, Bertha Johnson
Corn Grinding: Mary Johnson
Recorded at: Klagetoh, Arizona, April 21 and November 10, 1974
Tribe: Navajo
Format: Cassette

Navajo Skip Dance and Two-Step Songs
INDIAN HOUSE RECORDS IH 1503
Contents: 24 Navajo skip dance songs, 7 two-step songs
Singers: Boniface Bonnie, Autisdy Smith, M.D. Johnson, Roy Bonnie, Ben J. Johnson, Donald Deal, Bertha Bonnie, Stella Bonnie, Winnie Bonnie, Nellie Curley, Mary Deal Recorded at: Klagetoh, Arizona, March 2, 1968
Tribe: Navajo
Format: Cassette

Night and Daylight Yeibichei
INDIAN HOUSE RECORDS IH 1502
Contents: 10 Navajo Yeibichei songs (5 night Yeibichei , 5 daylight Yeibichei)
Singers: Boniface Bonnie, Autisdy Smith, M.D. Johnson, Roy Bonnie, Ben J. Johnson, Benny Roan Horse, Ted Bonnie, Donald Deal
Recorded at: Klagetoh, Arizona, March 2, 1968
Tribe: Navajo
Format: CD, Cassette
Notes: The Navajo Yeibichei is the public portion of a nine day healing ceremony performed only in the winter months. It is performed in order to help cure a patient suffering from eye trouble, ear trouble, or paralysis. This recording features old-style Yeibichei singing, and seldom-heard songs with rattle accompaniment.

Navajo Sway Songs
INDIAN HOUSE RECORDS IH 1501
Contents: 42 Navajo sway songs (from the Enemy Way Ceremony)
Singers: Boniface Bonnie, Autisdy Smith, Ben J. Johnson, Donald Deal, Stella
Bonnie, Winnie Bonnie, Nellie Curley, Mary Deal
Recorded at: Klagetoh, Arizona, February 25, 1968
Tribe: Navajo
Format: Cassette, LP

Nootka Music

Various Artists
Nootka Indian Music of the Pacific Northwest Coast
Smithsonian / Folkways 4524, Recorded: Live, Format: Cassette

Omaha Music

Omaha White Tail Singers
War Dancer - Pow-Wow Songs of the Omaha
CANYON RECORDS CR-6249, Tribe: Omaha, Recorded: Studio, Format:
Cassette

Paiute Music

Trejo, Judy
Circle Dance Songs of the Paiute & Shoshone
CANYON RECORDS CR-6283, Tribe: Paiute, Recorded: Studio, Format:
Cassette

Stick Game Songs of the Paiute
CANYON RECORDS CR-6284, Tribe: Paiute, Recorded: Studio, Format:
Cassette

Various Artists
War, Bear & Sun Dance Songs
CANYON RECORDS CR-6113, Tribe: Paiute, Recorded: Studio, Format:
Cassette

Papago – Pima Music

Mahone, Keith
Social Songs from the Pima Indians
CANYON RECORDS CR-6066, Tribe: Papago-Pima, Recorded: Studio, Format:
Cassette

Traditional Pima Dance Songs
CANYON RECORDS CR-8011, Tribe: Papago-Pima, Recorded: Studio, Format:
Cassette

98

Vol. 1, Traditional Papago Music
CANYON RECORDS CR-6084, Tribe: Papago-Pima, Recorded: Studio, Format: Cassette

Vol.,2, Papago Dance Songs
CANYON RECORDS CR-6098, Tribe: Papago-Pima, Recorded: Studio, Format: Cassette

Pawnee Music

Various Artists
Music of the Pawnee
Smithsonian / Folkways 4334, Recorded: Live, Format: Cassette

Picuris Music

Various Artists
Ditch-Cleaning and Picnic Songs Of Picuris Pueblo
INDIAN HOUSE RECORDS IH 1051
Contents: 5 ditch-cleaning songs and 5 picnic songs
Singer: Ramos Duran
Recorded at: Picuris Pueblo, New Mexico, September 11, 1966, and January 22, 1970 Tribe: Picuris Pueblo Format: Cassette, LP

Ponca Music

Ponca Indian Singers
Ponca War Dances
CANYON RECORDS CR-6143, Tribe: Ponca, Recorded: Studio, Format: Cassette

Various Artists
Pow Wow!
CANYON RECORDS CR-6088, Tribe: Ponca, Recorded: Studio, Format: Cassette

San Juan Music

Setima, Ben
Pueblo Indian Songs from San Juan
CANYON RECORDS CR-6065, Tribe: San Juan, Recorded: Studio, Format: Cassette

The San Juan Singers
The San Juan Singers - Navajo Skip Dance Songs
INDIAN HOUSE RECORDS IH 1521
Contents:: 13 Navajo skip dance songs
Singers: Thomas Blackhorse, Kenneth Benally, Stanley Benally Sr., Harry
Benally, Timothy Blackhorse, Jim Bitsilly, Paul Anderson
Recorded at: Waterflow, New Mexico, May 5, 1979
Tribe: Navajo
Format: Cassette, LP

The Tewa Indian Women's Choir of San Juan Pueblo
The Tewa Indian Women's Choir of San Juan Pueblo - Songs from the Tewa
Mass
INDIAN HOUSE RECORDS TWC 1
Contents: 4 Tewa songs for the Catholic Mass, Tewa versions Of Amazing Grace
and How Great Thou Art, 3 Ánge'in (traditional San Juan Pueblo spiritual songs)
Performers: Tewa Indian Women's Choir
Recorded at: San Juan Pueblo, New Mexico, April 26, 1994
Format: Cassette

Various Artists
Turtle Dance Songs of San Juan Pueblo
INDIAN HOUSE RECORDS IH 1101
Contents: 6 turtle dance songs
Singer: Joe M. Abeyta, Cipriano Garcia, Jerry Garcia, Peter Garcia, Carpio
Trujillo, John R. Trujillo
Recorded at: San Juan Pueblo, New Mexico, February 13, 1972
Tribe: San Juan Pueblo
Format: Cassette
The Turtle Dance of San Juan Pueblo is performed each year on December 26.
It is a winter solstice prayer dance for protection and long life for the community.
This recording features outstanding Pueblo singing by a group of six men,
accompanied by turtle shells, gourd rattles, and bells.
Cloud Dance Songs of San Juan Pueblo
INDIAN HOUSE RECORDS IH 1102
Contents: 6 cloud dance songs
Singer: Joe M. Abeyta, Cipriano Garcia, Jerry Garcia, Peter Garcia, Carpio
Trujillo, John R. Trujillo
Recorded at: San Juan Pueblo, New Mexico, February 27, 1972
Tribe: San Juan Pueblo
Format: Cassette

Seminole Music

Various Artists
Songs of the Seminole Indians of Florida
Smithsonian / Folkways 4383, Recorded: Live, Format: Cassette

Seneca Music

Various Artists
Seneca Social Dance Music
Smithsonian / Folkways 4072, Recorded: Live, Format: Cassette

Sioux Music

Eagle Tail Singers
Pow-Wow Songs Recorded Live!
CANYON RECORDS CR-16245, Tribe: Sioux, Recorded: Studio, Format:
Cassette

Fort Kipp Singers
Vol.1, At Fort Qu'Appelle
CANYON RECORDS CR-6079, Tribe: Sioux, Recorded: Studio, Format:
Cassette

Vol.2, Montana Grass Songs
CANYON RECORDS CR-6101, Tribe: Sioux, Recorded: Studio, Format:
Cassette

Vol.3, Fort Kipp Celebration
CANYON RECORDS CR-6152, Tribe: Sioux, Recorded: Studio, Format:
Cassette

Vol.4, Fort Kipp '77 Live
CANYON RECORDS CR-8034, Tribe: Sioux, Recorded: Studio, Format:
Cassette

Ironwood Singers
Sioux Songs
CANYON RECORDS CR-8030, Tribe: Sioux, Recorded: Studio, Format:
Cassette

Locke, Kevin
Love Songs Of The Lakota - Performed on Flute by Kevin Locke
INDIAN HOUSE RECORDS 4315
Contents: 12 traditional Lakota love songs
Recorded at: Storm Mountain, Black Hills, South Dakota, September 1-2, 1982
Tribe: Lakota Sioux
Format: CD, Cassette
Kevin Locke began studying Lakota flute many years ago. At an early age he
sought out tribal elders, and learned not only traditional love songs, but also the
history of each song. Traditionally, a love song can either be sung or played on
the flute. Recorded outdoors, next to a stream in the Black Hills of South Dakota,
this is Kevin's first published recording. It features 12 Lakota love songs played
on three different flutes. The recording contains extensive notes written by Kevin
Locke and Edward Wahpeconiah.

Pass Creek Singers
> *Pow-Wow Songs*
> CANYON RECORDS CR-16248, Tribe: Sioux, Recorded: Studio, Format: Cassette

Porcupine Singers
> *Vol.1, At Ring Thunder*
> CANYON RECORDS CR-8006, Tribe: Sioux, Recorded: Studio, Format: Cassette

> *Vol.2, Traditional Sioux Songs*
> CANYON RECORDS CR-8007, Tribe: Sioux, Recorded: Studio, Format: Cassette

> *Vol.3, Concert in Vermillion*
> CANYON RECORDS CR-8008, Tribe: Sioux, Recorded: Studio, Format: Cassette

> *Vol.4, At University of South Dakota*
> CANYON RECORDS CR-8010, Tribe: Sioux, Recorded: Studio, Format: Cassette

> *Vol.5, Rabbit Dance Songs, Part 1*
> CANYON RECORDS CR-6191, Tribe: Sioux, Recorded: Studio, Format: Cassette

> *Vol.6, Rabbit Dance Songs, Part 2*
> CANYON RECORDS CR-6192, Tribe: Sioux, Recorded: Studio, Format: Cassette

> *Vol.7, Remembering the Singer*
> CANYON RECORDS CR-16237, Tribe: Sioux, Recorded: Studio, Format: Cassette

> *Vol.8, Keep the Tradition*
> CANYON RECORDS CR-16238, Tribe: Sioux, Recorded: Studio, Format: Cassette

Rock Creek Singers
> *Pow-Wow Songs*
> CANYON RECORDS CR-8032, Tribe: Sioux, Recorded: Studio, Format: Cassette

Joseph Shields II (Jr.)
> *Wahancanka-Lakota Pipe & Ceremonial Songs*
> CANYON RECORDS CR-6285, Tribe: Sioux, Recorded: Studio, Format: Cassette

Various Artists
> *Music of the Sioux and Navajo*
> Smithsonian / Folkways 4401, Recorded: Live, Format: Cassette

Sioux Favorites
CANYON RECORDS CR-6059, Tribe: Sioux, Recorded: Studio, Format: Cassette

Songs of the Sioux
CANYON RECORDS CR-6062, Tribe: Sioux, Recorded: Studio, Format: Cassette

William Horncloud
Sioux Songs of War & Love
CANYON RECORDS CR-6150, Tribe: Sioux, Recorded: Studio, Format: Cassette

Sioux Rabbit Dance Songs
CANYON RECORDS CR-6081, Tribe: Sioux, Recorded: Studio, Format: Cassette

Taos Music

Various Artists
Taos Pueblo Tribal Songs
INDIAN HOUSE RECORDS SC 205
Contents: 10 round dance songs, 2 war dance songs
Performers: Joe Trinidad Archuleta, George Archuleta, Joe Suazo
Recorded at: Recorded at Taos Pueblo, NM, July 27, 1953.
Tribe: Taos Pueblo
Format: Cassette

Umatilla Music

Umatilla Tribal Singers
Umatilla Tribal Songs
CANYON RECORDS CR-6131, Tribe: Umatilla, Recorded: Studio, Format: Cassette

Warm Springs Music

Various Artists
Songs of the Warm Springs Indian
CANYON RECORDS CR-6123, Tribe: Warm Springs, Recorded: Studio, Format: Cassette

Washington, Joe Lummi
Stick Game Songs
CANYON RECORDS CR-6124, Tribe: Warm Springs, Recorded: Studio, Format: Cassette

Yakima Music

Selam & Hill
Songs of a Yakima Encampment Treaty of 1855
CANYON RECORDS CR-6129, Tribe: Yakima, Recorded: Studio, Format:
Cassette

Yakima Nation Singers
Yakima Nation of Satus Longhouse
CANYON RECORDS CR-6126, Tribe: Yakima, Recorded: Studio, Format:
Cassette

Yaqui Music

Molina & Valencia
Yaqui Pascola Music of Arizona
CANYON RECORDS CR-7998, Tribe: Yaqui, Recorded: Studio, Format:
Cassette

Various Artists
Indian Music of Northwest Mexico
CANYON RECORDS CR-8001, Tribe: Yaqui, Recorded: Studio, Format:
Cassette

Music of the Pascola and Deer Dance
CANYON RECORDS CR-6099, Tribe: Yaqui, Recorded: Studio, Format:
Cassette

Yaqui Ritual & Festive Music
CANYON RECORDS CR-6140, Tribe: Yaqui, Recorded: Studio, Format:
Cassette

Zuni Music

Setima, Ben
Zuni
CANYON RECORDS CR-6060, Tribe: Zuni, Recorded: Studio, Format: Cassette

Various Artists
Zuni Fair - Live
INDIAN HOUSE RECORDS IH 1401
Contents: Harvest Dances by Tekapo Village, Navajo Songs and Zuni Legend
Song by the Zuni Olla Maidens, Hopi Butterfly Dance and Zuni Butterfly Dance
by Pescado Village
Recorded live at: the Zuni McKinley County Fair at Zuni, New Mexico, August 27-
29, 1971
Tribe: Zuni Pueblo
Format: Cassette

Chicken Scratch Music

American Indians
>*Vol.3*
>CANYON RECORDS CR-8072, Recorded: Studio, Format: Cassette

Braves
>*Vol.1*
>CANYON RECORDS CR-8079, Recorded: Studio, Format: Cassette
>
>*Vol.2*
>CANYON RECORDS CR-8086, Recorded: Studio, Format: Cassette
>
>*Vol.3*
>CANYON RECORDS CR-8091, Recorded: Studio, Format: Cassette
>
>*Vol.4*
>CANYON RECORDS CR-8096, Recorded: Studio, Format: Cassette
>
>*Vol.5*
>CANYON RECORDS CR-8112, Recorded: Studio, Format: Cassette

Cisco Band
>*Vol.2*
>CANYON RECORDS CR-8058, Recorded: Studio, Format: Cassette
>
>*Vol.3*
>CANYON RECORDS CR-8073, Recorded: Studio, Format: Cassette
>
>*Vol.4*
>CANYON RECORDS CR-8089, Recorded: Studio, Format: Cassette

Desert Horizon
>*Sunset to Sunrise*
>CANYON RECORDS CR-8116, Recorded: Studio, Format: Cassette

Desert Suns
>*Vol. 1*
>CANYON RECORDS CR-8105, Recorded: Studio, Format: Cassette
>
>*Vol. 2*
>CANYON RECORDS CR-8108, Recorded: Studio, Format: Cassette

El Conjunto Murrietta
>*Chicken Scratch!*
>CANYON RECORDS CR-6085, Recorded: Studio, Format: Cassette
>Re-release of Canyon's first Chicken Scratch album

Friends
>*His Music Lives On*
>CANYON RECORDS CR-8099, Recorded: Studio, Format: Cassette

Joaquin Brothers
Plays Polkas & Chotis!
CANYON RECORDS CR-6139, Recorded: Studio, Format: Cassette

Gu-Achi Fiddlers
Vol.1, O'odham Fiddle Music
CANYON RECORDS CR-8082, Recorded: Studio, Format: Cassette

Vol.2, O'odham Fiddle Music
CANYON RECORDS CR-8092, Recorded: Studio, Format: Cassette

Joe Miguel and the Blood Brothers
Vol.1
CANYON RECORDS CR-8052, Recorded: Studio, Format: Cassette

Vol.2
CANYON RECORDS CR-8068, Recorded: Studio, Format: Cassette

Vol.3
CANYON RECORDS CR-8077, Recorded: Studio, Format: Cassette

Jose's & Gomez Band
Papago Chicken Scratch
CANYON RECORDS CR-8074, Recorded: Studio, Format: Cassette

Los Papagos Molinas
Vol.1 Superscratch Kings
CANYON RECORDS CR-6128, Recorded: Studio, Format: Cassette
Re-release of a classic Chicken Scratch album.

Vol.5
CANYON RECORDS CR-8063, Recorded: Studio, Format: Cassette

Vol.6
CANYON RECORDS CR-8087, Recorded: Studio, Format: Cassette

Papago Express
Vol.1
CANYON RECORDS CR-8076, Recorded: Studio, Format: Cassette

Papago Raiders
Vol.1
CANYON RECORDS CR-8057, Recorded: Studio, Format: Cassette

Vol.2
CANYON RECORDS CR-8064, Recorded: Studio, Format: Cassette

Vol.3
CANYON RECORDS CR-8070, Recorded: Studio, Format: Cassette

Vol.4
CANYON RECORDS CR-8081, Recorded: Studio, Format: Cassette

Vol.5
CANYON RECORDS CR-8090, Recorded: Studio, Format: Cassette

Papago Indian Band
Papago Indian Band
CANYON RECORDS CR-8075, Recorded: Studio, Format: Cassette

Papago Sunliners
Vol.1
CANYON RECORDS CR-8059, Recorded: Studio, Format: Cassette

Vol.3
CANYON RECORDS CR-8065, Recorded: Studio, Format: Cassette

Pima Express
Always Be Your Friend
CANYON RECORDS CR-8107, Recorded: Studio, Format: Cassette

From the Past to the Future
CANYON RECORDS CR-8109, Recorded: Studio, Format: Cassette
Nothing Special
CANYON RECORDS CR-8115, Recorded: Studio, Format: Cassette

Together We'll Fade Away
CANYON RECORDS CR-8113, Recorded: Studio, Format: Cassette

Voices Upon the Wind
CANYON RECORDS CR-8117, Recorded: Studio, Format: Cassette

Red Feather Band
Chicken Scratch & O'odham Country
CANYON RECORDS CR-8106, Recorded: Studio, Format: Cassette

Specialty Songs
CANYON RECORDS CR-8111, Recorded: Studio, Format: Cassette

Renegades
Renegades
CANYON RECORDS CR-8103, Recorded: Studio, Format: Cassette

San Xavier Fiddle Band
Old Time Fiddle Music
CANYON RECORDS CR-8085, Recorded: Studio, Format: Cassette

Santan
Vol.1, Pima Chicken Scratch
CANYON RECORDS CR-8051, Recorded: Studio, Format: Cassette

Vol.2
CANYON RECORDS CR-8056, Recorded: Studio, Format: Cassette

Vol.3
CANYON RECORDS CR-8061, Recorded: Studio, Format: Cassette

Simon & Friends
Vol.1
CANYON RECORDS CR-8102, Recorded: Studio, Format: Cassette

Southern Scratch
Vol.1
CANYON RECORDS CR-8093, Recorded: Studio, Format: Cassette

Vol.2
CANYON RECORDS CR-8094, Recorded: Studio, Format: Cassette

Vol.3 Em-we:hejed For All of You
CANYON RECORDS CR-8097, Recorded: Studio, Format: Cassette

Vol.4, Chicken Scratch Christmas
CANYON RECORDS CR-8101, Recorded: Studio, Format: Cassette

Vol.5 Piast Tas (Fiesta Time)
CANYON RECORDS CR-8110, Recorded: Studio, Format: Cassette

T.O.Combo
Vol.1
CANYON RECORDS CR-8083, Recorded: Studio, Format: Cassette

Vol.2
CANYON RECORDS CR-8100, Recorded: Studio, Format: Cassette

Vol.3, T.O. Forever
CANYON RECORDS CR-8114, Recorded: Studio, Format: Cassette

The Legends
The Legends
CANYON RECORDS CR-8060, Recorded: Studio, Format: Cassette

The Santa Rosa Band
Vol.2
CANYON RECORDS CR-8062, Recorded: Studio, Format: Cassette

Vol.3
CANYON RECORDS CR-8071, Recorded: Studio, Format: Cassette

Vol.4
CANYON RECORDS CR-8084, Recorded: Studio, Format: Cassette

Vol.5
CANYON RECORDS CR-8098, Recorded: Studio, Format: Cassette

Vol.6
CANYON RECORDS CR-8104, Recorded: Studio, Format: Cassette

The Tribesmen
Pima Chicken Scratch
CANYON RECORDS CR-8069, Recorded: Studio, Format: Cassette

Thee Express
Vol.2
CANYON RECORDS CR-8078, Recorded: Studio, Format: Cassette

Vol.3
CANYON RECORDS CR-8095, Recorded: Studio, Format: Cassette

Various Artists
Chicken Scratch Fiesta
CANYON RECORDS CR-8055, Recorded: Studio, Format: Cassette

Verton Jackson Combo
Vol.1
CANYON RECORDS CR-8066, Recorded: Studio, Format: Cassette

Virgil Jose & Friends
Vol.1
CANYON RECORDS CR-8067, Recorded: Studio, Format: Cassette

Vol.2
CANYON RECORDS CR-8080, Recorded: Studio, Format: Cassette

Vol.3
CANYON RECORDS CR-8088, Recorded: Studio, Format: Cassette

Peyote Ritual Music

Armstrong, Alfred
Indian Lord's Prayer Songs
CANYON RECORDS CR-8025, Recorded: Studio, Format: Cassette

Aunguoe, James
Kiowa Peyote Ritual Songs
INDIAN HOUSE RECORDS SC 549
Contents: 15 peyote ritual songs
Singers: James Aunguoe
Tribe: Kiowa
Format: Cassette

Denny, Jr., Bill
Vol.1, Intertribal Peyote Chants
CANYON RECORDS CR-8027, Recorded: Studio, Format: Cassette

Vol.2, Intertribal Peyote Chants
CANYON RECORDS CR-8028, Recorded: Studio, Format: Cassette

Vol.3, Intertribal Peyote Chants
CANYON RECORDS CR-8029, Recorded: Studio, Format: Cassette

Vol.4, Intertribal Peyote Chants
CANYON RECORDS CR-8035, Recorded: Studio, Format: Cassette

Vol.5, Intertribal Peyote Chants
CANYON RECORDS CR-8036, Recorded: Studio, Format: Cassette

Vol.6, Intertribal Peyote Chants
CANYON RECORDS CR-8038, Recorded: Studio, Format: Cassette

Barker & Butler
Vol.2, Peyote Songs
CANYON RECORDS CR-8021, Recorded: Studio, Format: Cassette

Daukei & Chester
Peyote Early Morning Chants
CANYON RECORDS CR-6158, Recorded: Studio, Format: Cassette

Dupoint & Tofpi
Kiowa Peyote Songs
CANYON RECORDS CR-6307, Recorded: Studio, Format: Cassette

Duran, Jr., Thomas
Connection to Mother Earth
CANYON RECORDS CR-6316, Recorded: Studio, Format: Cassette

Life Giver
CANYON RECORDS CR-6343, Recorded: Studio, Format: Cassette

Guy and Allen
Peyote Brothers
SOAR 151, Recorded: Studio, Format: CD, Cassette

Peyote Canyon
SOAR 129, Recorded: Studio, Format: CD, Cassette

Peyote Medicine
SOAR 138, Recorded: Studio, Format: CD, Cassette

Peyote Strength
SOAR 161, Recorded: Studio, Format: CD, Cassette

Guy, Jr., Paul & Teddy Allen
Diné Peyote Songs
CANYON RECORDS CR-6295, Recorded: Studio, Format: Cassette

James and Nez
Peyote Blessing
SOAR 159, Recorded: Studio, Format: CD, Cassette

Nez, Billie
Peyote Songs from Navaholand
SOAR 114, Recorded: Studio, Format: CD, Cassette

James and Nez
Peyote Blessing
SOAR 159, Recorded: Studio, Format: CD, Cassette

Paul Guy, Jr. & Paul Guy, Sr.
My Father's Chapel
CANYON RECORDS CR-6294, Recorded: Studio, Format: Cassette

Kaulaity & Cozad
Kiowa Peyote Songs
CANYON RECORDS CR-6144, Recorded: Studio, Format: Cassette

Knight, Jimmy
Healing Songs in Navajo
CANYON RECORDS CR-6308, Recorded: Studio, Format: Cassette

Navajo Healing Songs
CANYON RECORDS CR-6330, Recorded: Studio, Format: Cassette

Parker Singers
Vol.1, Peyote Songs from Rocky Boy
CANYON RECORDS CR-8022, Recorded: Studio, Format: Cassette

Vol.2, Peyote Songs from Rocky Boy
CANYON RECORDS CR-8023, Recorded: Studio, Format: Cassette

Vol.3, Peyote Songs from Rocky Boy
CANYON RECORDS CR-8024, Recorded: Studio, Format: Cassette

Pomani & Thomas Duran Jr.
Connection to Mother Earth
CANYON RECORDS CR-6316, Recorded: Studio, Format: Cassette

Go Protect Us
CANYON RECORDS CR-6336, Recorded: Studio, Format: Cassette

Sacred Medicine Guide Us Home
CANYON RECORDS CR-6359, Recorded: Studio, Format: Cassette

Primeaux & Mike
Vol.1, Peyote Songs
CANYON RECORDS CR-16301, Recorded: Studio, Format: Cassette

Vol.2, Peyote & Healing Songs
CANYON RECORDS CR-16302, Recorded: Studio, Format: Cassette

Vol.3, Peyote Songs
CANYON RECORDS CR-16303, Recorded: Studio, Format: Cassette

Vol.4, Walk in Beauty: Healing Songs
CANYON RECORDS CR-16304, Recorded: Studio, Format: Cassette

Vol.5, Peyote Songs
CANYON RECORDS CR-16305, Recorded: Studio, Format: Cassette

Vol. 6, Sacred Path
CANYON RECORDS CR-6306, Recorded: Studio, Format: Cassette

Vol. 7, Peyote Songs of the Native American Church
CANYON RECORDS CR-6309, Recorded: Studio, Format: Cassette

Vol. 8, Gatherning of Voices
CANYON RECORDS CR-6310, Recorded: Studio, Format: Cassette

Vol. 9, Live in Harmony
CANYON RECORDS CR-6313, Recorded: Studio, Format: Cassette

Vol. 10, Evolution: Generation to Generation
CANYON RECORDS CR-6314, Recorded: Studio, Format: Cassette

Vol. 11, Bless the People
CANYON RECORDS CR-6317, Recorded: Studio, Format: Cassette

Vol. 12, Hours Before Dawn
CANYON RECORDS CR-6342, Recorded: Studio, Format: Cassette

Secody, Eli
The Following Generation
CANYON RECORDS CR-6348, Recorded: Studio, Format: Cassette

Shields, Joe III
Vol. 1, Songs of the Peyote Road
CANYON RECORDS CR-6311, Recorded: Studio, Format: Cassette

Vol. 2, Songs of the Peyote Road
CANYON RECORDS CR-6312, Recorded: Studio, Format: Cassette

Various Artists
Cheyenne Peyote Songs - Volume 1
INDIAN HOUSE RECORDS IH 2201
Contents: 25 peyote songs
Singers: Arthur Madbull, Lee R. Chouteau, Toby Starr, Allen Bushyhead
Recorded at: Calumet, Oklahoma, May 15, 1975
Tribe: Cheyenne
Format: Cassette, LP

Cheyenne Peyote Songs - Volume 2
INDIAN HOUSE RECORDS IH 2202
Contents: 24 peyote songs
Singers: Arthur Madbull, Lee R. Chouteau, Toby Starr, Allen Bushyhead
Recorded at: Calumet, Oklahoma, May 15, 1975--Continued from INDIAN
HOUSE RECORDS IH 2201
Tribe: Cheyenne
Format: Cassette, LP

Comanche Peyote Songs - Volume 1
INDIAN HOUSE RECORDS IH 2401
Contents: 24 Comanche peyote morning songs
Singers: Roy Simmons, Joy Niedo, Roy Wockmetooah, Roe Kahrahrah, Mary
Poafpybitty, Jessie Poahway, Ida Wockmetooah
Recorded at: Apache, Oklahoma, April 30, 1969
Tribe: Comanche
Format: Cassette

Comanche Peyote Songs - Volume 2
INDIAN HOUSE RECORDS IH 2402
Contents: 23 Comanche peyote morning songs
Singers: Roy Simmons, Joy Niedo, Roy Wockmetooah, Roe Kahrahrah, Mary
Poafpybitty, Jessie Poahway, Ida Wockmetooah
Recorded at: Apache, Oklahoma, April 30, 1969--Continued from INDIAN
HOUSE RECORDS IH
Tribe: Comanche
Format: Cassette, LP

Kiowa and Comanche Peyote Songs
INDIAN HOUSE RECORDS SC 591
Contents: 13 songs
Singer: Nelson Big Bow

Recorded at: Crow Agency, Montana, August 24, 1966
Tribe: Kiowa, Comanche
Format: Cassette

Kiowa and Kiowa-Apache Peyote Ritual Songs
INDIAN HOUSE RECORDS SC 548
Contents: 20 peyote songs
Singers: Emmett Williams, Nathan Doyebi, Edgar Gouladdle, Nelson Big Bow
Tribe: Kiowa, Kiowa-Apache
Format: Cassette

Kiowa-Comanche Peyote Songs
INDIAN HOUSE RECORDS SC 507
Contents: 23 peyote songs
Singers: Nelson Big Bow, Edgar Gouladdle, Harding Big Bow, Walter Ahhaity
Tribe: Kiowa, Comanche
Format: Cassette

Kiowa Peyote Ritual Songs
INDIAN HOUSE RECORDS SC 580
Contents: 22 songs (including the Opening, Midnight, Water, and Closing songs)
Singers: James Aunguoe, Ernest Redbird, Allen Tsontokoy, Francis Tsontokoy,
OINDIAN HOUSE RECORDS SCar Tahlo
Tribe: Kiowa
Format: Cassette

Kiowa Peyote Ritual Songs
INDIAN HOUSE RECORDS SC 590
Contents:15 songs
Singer: Edward Hummingbird
Recorded at: Crow Agency, Montana, August 24, 1966
Tribe: Kiowa
Format: Cassette

Navajo Peyote Ceremonial Songs - Volume 1
INDIAN HOUSE RECORDS IH 1541
Contents: 24 Navajo peyote ceremonial songs
Singers: Wilson Aronilth Jr., Hanson Ashley
Recorded at: Wheatfield Arizona, October 20, 1979
Tribe: Navajo
Format: CD, Cassette An invaluable introduction to the Navajo way of prayer in
the Native American Church. Extensive notes written by Wilson Aronilth, Jr.
explain the history, beliefs, and music of the Navajo peyote way. English
translations are provided. These exquisite songs are accompanied by a gourd
rattle and water drum.

Navajo Peyote Ceremonial Songs - Volume 2
INDIAN HOUSE RECORDS IH 1542
Contents: 24 Navajo peyote ceremonial songs
Singers: Wilson Aronilth Jr., Hanson Ashley
Recorded at: Wheatfield Arizona, October 20, 1979--Continued from IH 1541
Tribe: Navajo   Format: Cassette

Navajo Peyote Ceremonial Songs - Volume 3
INDIAN HOUSE RECORDS IH 1543
Contents: 24 Navajo peyote ceremonial songs
Singers: Wilson Aronilth Jr., Hanson Ashley
Recorded at: Wheatfield Arizona, October 20, 1979-- Continued from IH 1542
Tribe: Navajo
Format: Cassette

Navajo Peyote Ceremonial Songs - Volume 4
INDIAN HOUSE RECORDS IH 1544
Contents: 24 Navajo peyote ceremonial songs
Singers: Wilson Aronilth Jr., Hanson Ashley
Recorded at: Wheatfield Arizona, October 20, 1979-- Continued from IH 1543
Tribe: Navajo
Format: Cassette

Old Peyote Songs
CANYON RECORDS CR-6054, Recorded: Studio, Format: Cassette

Ponca Peyote Songs - Volume 1
INDIAN HOUSE RECORDS IH 2005
Contents: 28 Ponca peyote songs
Singers: Harry Buffalohead, James Clark, Joe H. Rush, Franklin Smith, Sylvester Warrior
Recorded at: Ponca City, Oklahoma, April 6, 1971
Tribe: Ponca
Format: Cassette, LP

Ponca Peyote Songs - Volume 2
INDIAN HOUSE RECORDS IH 2006
Contents: 24 Ponca peyote songs
Singers: Harry Buffalohead, James Clark, Joe H. Rush, Franklin Smith, Sylvester Warrior
Recorded at: Ponca City, Oklahoma, April 6, 1971--Continued from INDIAN HOUSE RECORDS IH 2005
Tribe: Ponca
Format: Cassette, LP

Ponca Peyote Songs - Volume 3
INDIAN HOUSE RECORDS IH 2007
Contents: 24 Ponca peyote songs
Singers: Harry Buffalohead, James Clark, Joe H. Rush, Franklin Smith, Sylvester Warrior
Recorded at: Recorded at Ponca City, Oklahoma, April 6, 1971--Continued from INDIAN HOUSE IH 2006
Tribe: Ponca
Format: Cassette, LP

Songs of the Native American Church
INDIAN HOUSE RECORDS 4379
Contents: 24 peyote songs of various tribes
Singers: Rev. Joseph M. Shields Sr., assisted by Duane L Shields Sr.
Recorded at: Lake Andes, South Dakota, June 29, 1979
Format: Cassette

Yankton Sioux Peyote Songs - Volume 1
INDIAN HOUSE RECORDS 4371
Contents: 24 peyote songs
Singers: Joe Abdo Sr., Quentin Bruguier, Lorenzo Dion, Asa Primeaux Sr.,
Francis Primeaux, Duane Shields, Joseph Shields Sr.
Recorded at: Lake Andes, South Dakota, July 6, 1976
Tribe: Yankton Sioux Format: Cassette, LP

Yankton Sioux Peyote Songs - Volume 2
INDIAN HOUSE RECORDS 4372
Contents: 24 peyote songs (including the original harmonized Sioux peyote
songs)
Singers: Joe Abdo Sr., Quentin Bruguier, Lorenzo Dion, Asa Primeaux Sr.,
Francis Primeaux, Duane Shields, Joseph Shields Sr., Philomene Dion
Recorded at: Recorded at Lake Andes, South Dakota, July 6, 1976.--Continued
from INDIAN HOUSE RECORDS 4371
Tribe: Yankton Sioux
Format: Cassette, LP

Yankton Sioux Peyote Songs - Volume 3
INDIAN HOUSE RECORDS 4373
Contents: 20 peyote songs
Singers: Joe Abdo Sr., Quentin Bruguier, Lorenzo Dion, Asa Primeaux Sr.,
Francis Primeaux, Duane Shields, Joseph Shields Sr., Philomene Dion
Recorded at: Lake Andes, South Dakota, July 6, 1976.--Continued from INDIAN
HOUSE RECORDS 4372
Tribe: Yankton Sioux
Format: Cassette, LP

Yankton Sioux Peyote Songs - Volume 4
INDIAN HOUSE RECORDS 4374
Contents: 24 peyote songs
Singers: Joe Abdo Sr., Quentin Bruguier, Lorenzo Dion, Asa Primeaux Sr.,
Francis Primeaux, Duane Shields, Joseph Shields Sr., Philomene Dion
Recorded at: Lake Andes, South Dakota, July 6, 1976.--Continued from INDIAN
HOUSE RECORDS 4373
Tribe: Yankton Sioux
Format: Cassette, LP

Yankton Sioux Peyote Songs - Volume 5
INDIAN HOUSE RECORDS 4375
Contents: 24 peyote songs
Singers: Rev. Joseph M. Shields Sr., Joseph Shields Jr., Lorenzo Dion, Joe
Abdo Sr., Duane L. Shields Sr., Philomene Dion
Recorded at: Lake Andes, South Dakota, June 29, 1979
Tribe: Yankton Sioux
Format: Cassette, LP

Yankton Sioux Peyote Songs - Volume 6
INDIAN HOUSE RECORDS 4376
Contents: 24 peyote songs
Singers: Rev. Joseph M. Shields Sr., Joseph Shields Jr., Lorenzo Dion, Joe
Abdo Sr., Duane L. Shields Sr., Philomene Dion
Recorded at: Lake Andes, South Dakota, June 29, 1979--Continued from INDIAN
HOUSE RECORDS 4375
Tribe: Yankton Sioux
Format: Cassette, LP

Yankton Sioux Peyote Songs - Volume 7
INDIAN HOUSE RECORDS 4377
Contents: 24 peyote songs
Singers: Rev. Joseph M. Shields Sr., Joseph Shields Jr., Lorenzo Dion, Joe
Abdo Sr., Duane L. Shields Sr., Philomene Dion
Recorded at: Lake Andes, South Dakota, June 29, 1979--Continued from INDIAN
HOUSE RECORDS 4376
Tribe: Yankton Sioux
Format: Cassette, LP

Yankton Sioux Peyote Songs - Volume 8
INDIAN HOUSE RECORDS 4378
Contents: 28 peyote songs
Singers: Rev. Joseph M. Shields Sr., Joseph Shields Jr., Lorenzo Dion, Joe
Abdo Sr., Duane L. Shields Sr., Philomene Dion
Recorded at: Lake Andes, South Dakota, June 29, 1979--Continued from INDIAN
HOUSE RECORDS 4377
Tribe: Yankton Sioux
Format: Cassette, LP

Van Horn, Barker & Clark
Vol.1, Peyote Prayer Songs
CANYON RECORDS CR-8018, Recorded: Studio, Format: Cassette

Vol.2, Peyote Prayer Songs
CANYON RECORDS CR-8019, Recorded: Studio, Format: Cassette

Wildcat Peak
Vol.1, Navajo Morning Peyote Songs
CANYON RECORDS CR-6159, Recorded: Studio, Format: Cassette

Vol.2, Peyote Songs
CANYON RECORDS CR-8014, Recorded: Studio, Format: Cassette

Vol.3, Morning Peyote Songs
CANYON RECORDS CR-8015, Recorded: Studio, Format: Cassette

Vol.4, Morning Peyote Songs
CANYON RECORDS CR-8016, Recorded: Studio, Format: Cassette

Vol.5, Peyote Songs
CANYON RECORDS CR-8037, Recorded: Studio, Format: Cassette

Wildcat Peak Youth
36 Navajo Morning Peyote Songs
CANYON RECORDS CR-8026, Recorded: Studio, Format: Cassette

How to order recordings

Music Café distributes all recordings contained in this book.
Titles can easily be ordered directly as follows:

Phone your order at (505) 984-9646

FAX your order at (505) 984-0647

Mail your order request to Music Café, PO Box 24259, Santa Fe, NM 87502

Email your order request to nativemusicdirectory@hotmail.com

Indicate the title, record label, and catalogue number. Our staff will provide you with the current price and can give you detailed shipping information for your convenience.

For additional information from record labels:

Arbor Records, Ltd.
49 Henderson Hwy
Winnipeg, Manitoba, Canada
R2L 1K9
Phone:(204) 663-0150
Fax: (204) 663-0140
Toll Free: 1-888-663-0651
email: info@arborrecords.com
website: www.arborrecords.com

Canyon Records Productions
3131 W. Clarendon Avenue
Phoenix, Arizona 85017
Phone: (800) 268-1141
FAX: (602) 279-9233
email: canyon@canyonrecords.com
website: www.canyonrecords.com

Indian House Records
PO Box 472
Taos, New Mexico 87571
Phone: 505-776-2953
FAX: 505-776-280
email: music@indianhouse.com
website: www.indianhouse.com

Smithsonian / Folkways Recordings
Smithsonian Folkways Mail Order
Smithsonian Folkways Recordings
Dept. 0607
Washington, DC 20073-0607
Phone: 1-800-410-9815
FAX: 1-800-853-9511 (International (202 275-1165)
email: folkways@aol.com
website: www.folkways.si.edu

128

Sunshine Records
>275 Selkirk Avenue
Winnipeg, MB
Canada, R2W 2L5
Phone: 1-800-307-8057
FAX: 1-204-582-8397
email: sunrec@total.net
website: www.sunshinerecords.com

Sweet Grass Records
>Sweet Grass Records
Box 23022 Saskatoon
Saskatchewan Canada S7J 5H3
Phone (306)343-7053
Toll free 1(877)755-1727
email: info@sweetgrassrecords.com
website: www.sweetgrassrecords.com

SOAR - Sound of America Records
>5200 Constitution NE
Albuquerque, NM 87110
Phone (505)-268-6110
Toll free1- 800-890-SOAR
FAX: (505)-268-0237
website: www.soundofamerica.com

Native American Radio Stations

Alaska

KBBI 890 AM	3913 Kachemak Way Homer, AK 99603	**Phone:** 907-235-7721 **Fax:** 907-235-2357 **E-mail:** kbbidev@xyz.net
KBRW 680 AM	1695 Okpik Street PO Box 109 Barrow, AK 99723	**Phone:** 907-852-6811 **Fax:** 907-852-2274 **E-Mail:** kbrw@barrow.com
KCUK 88.1 FM	Kashunaniut School Dist. 985 KSD Way Chevak, AK 99563	**Phone:** 907-858-7014 **Fax:** 907-858-7279
KDLG 670 AM	670 Seward Highway PO Box 670 Dillingham, AK 99576	**Phone:** 907-842-5281 **Fax:** 907-842-5645
KDLL 91.9 FM	Pickle Hill Public Broadcasting Inc. PO Box 2111 Kenai, AK 99611	**Phone:** 907-283-8433
KNBA_ 90.3 FM	Koahnic Broadcast Corp. 719 East 11th Ave. Suite C Anchorage, AK 99501	**Phone:** 907-258-8880 **Fax:** 907-258-8803 **E-mail:** knba@knba.org
KNSA 930 AM	P.O. Box 178 Unalakleet, AK 99684	**Phone:** 907-624-3101
KOTZ 720 AM	Kotzebue Broadcasting, Inc. PO Box 78 Kotzebue, AK 99752	**Phone:** 907-442-3434/3435 **Fax:** 907-442-2292
KRBD 105.9 FM	Rainbird Community Braodcasting Corporation 123 Stedman St Ketchikan, AK 99901	**Phone:** 907-225-9655 **E-mail:** diane@krbd.org
KSDP 830 AM	PO Box 328 Sand Point, AK 99661	**Phone:** 907-383-5737 **Fax:** 907-383-5271
KSKO 870 AM	PO Box 70 Mile 389, Iditarod Trail McGrath, AK 99627	**Phone:** 907-524-3001 **Fax:** 907-524-3436
KUHB 91.9 FM	School Dist Board of Education 930 Tolstoi St Box 905 St Paul Island, AK 99660	**Phone:** 907-546-2254 **E-mail:** kuhb@yahoo.com

KYUK
640 AM

Pouch 468
237 Radio Street
Bethel, AK 99559

Phone: 907-543-3131
Fax: 907-543-3130

KZPA
900 AM

Gwandak Public
Broadcasting Inc.
PO Box 50
Fort Yukon, AK 99740-

Phone: 907-662-8255
Fax: 907-662-8255

Arizona
KGHR
91.5 FM

PO Box 160
Tuba City, AZ 86045

Phone: 928-283-5555
Fax: 928-283-6604

KNNB
88.1, 89.9, 99.1 FM

Apache Radio
Broadcasting Corp. P. O.
BOX 700
Whiteriver, AZ 85941

Phone: 928-338-5229
Fax: 928-338-1744

KRMH
89.7 FM

Red Mesa HSD
HC 6100 Box 40
Teec Nos Pos, AZ 86514

Phone: 928-656-3511

KTNN
660 AM

PO Box 2569
Window Rock, AZ 86515

Phone: 928-871-2582
Fax: 928-871-3479
E-mail: ktnn@cia-g.com

KUYI
88.1 FM

PO Box 169
Hotevilla, AZ 86030

Phone: 928-734-5894
Fax: 928-734-9520
E-mail: RadioHopi@aol.com

KWRK
96.1 FM

PO Box 2569
Window Rock, AZ

Phone: 928-871-2582
Fax: 928-871-3479
E-mail: ktnn@cia-g.com

California
KIDE
91.3 FM

Hoopa Valley
Telecommunications Corp.
P.O.Box 1220 Hoopa, CA
95546

Phone: 530-625-4245
Fax: 530-625-4046

KPFA
94.1 FM

1929 Matin Luther King, Jr
Way
Berkeley, CA 94704

Phone: 510-848-6767
Fax: 310-848-3812
E-mail: kpfastaff@yahoo.com

KTQX
90.5 FM

Radio Billingue
5005 E Belmont Ave.
Fresno, CA

Phone: 800-200-5758
Fax: 559-455-5778
E-mail: rhbw65c@prodigy.com

Colorado
KGNU
88.5 FM

P.O. Box 885
Boulder, CO 80306

Phone: 303-449-4885
Fax: 303-447-9955

KRZA 88.7 FM	528 Ninth Street Alamosa, CO 81101	**Phone:** 719-589-9057 **Fax:** 719-589-9258 **E-Mail:** david@krza.com
KSJD 91.5 FM	33057 Highway 160 Mancos, CO 81328	**Phone:** 970-565-9121 **Fax:** 970-565-8450
KSUT 91.3 FM	PO Box 737 Ignacio, CO 81137	**Phone:** 970-563-0255 **Fax:** 970-563-0399 **E-Mail:** ksut@ksut.org
KUVO 89.3 FM	PO Box 11111 Denver, CO 80211	**Phone:** 303-480-9272 **Fax:** 303-291-0757 **E-Mail:** info@kuvo.org

Idaho

KISU 91.1 FM	Idaho State University Box 8310 Pocatello, ID 83209	**Phone:** 208-236-2688 **Fax:** 208-236-4600 **E-mail:** kisu_fm91@hotmail.com

Illinois

WLUW 88.7 FM	**Phone:** 312-915-6558 **E-mail:** 1wluwradio@wluw.org	**Phone:** 312-915-6558 **E-mail:** 1wluwradio@wluw.org

Michigan

WLNZ 89.7 FM	400 North Capitol Suite 001 Lansing, MI	**Phone:** 517-483-1710 **Fax:** 517-483-1849 **E-mail:** dave_downing@lansing.cc.mi.us

Minnesota

KAXE 91.7 FM	1841 East Highway 169 Grand Rapids, MN 55744-3398	**Phone:** 218-326-1234 **Fax:** 218-326-1235 **E-mail:** comments@kaxe.org

Montana

KGVA 88.1 FM	PO Box 159 Ft. Belknap College Harlem, MT 59526	**Phone:** 406-353-4556 **Fax:** 406-353-2898

Nebraska

KZUM 89.3 FM	941 "O" Street Suite 1025 Lincoln, NE 68508	**Phone:** 402-474-5086 **Fax:** 402-474-5091 **E-mail:** KZUMRadio@aol.com

New Mexico

KABR 1500 AM	PO Box 907 Magdalena, NM 87825	**Phone:** 505-854-2641 **Fax:** 505-854-2545 **E-Mail:** sarah@alamo.bia.edu

KCIE 90.5 FM	PO Box 603 Dulce, NM 87528	**Phone:** 505-759-3681 **Fax::** 505-759-9140
KGLP 91.7 FM	University of New Mexico Gallup 200 College Road Gallup, NM 87301	**Phone:** 505-863-7625 **Fax:** 505-863-7532 **E-Mail:** jhoover@gallup.net
KSHI 90.9 FM	PO Box 339 Zuni, NM 87327	**Phone:** 505-782-4144 **Fax:** 505-782-5069
KTDB 89.7 FM	PO Box 40 Pinehill, NM 87357	**Phone:** 505-775-3215 **Fax:** 505-775-3551 **E-Mail:** bernieb897@aol.com
KUNM 89.9 FM	The University of New Mexico Albuquerque, NM 87131-1011	**Phone:** 505-277-4806 **Fax:** 505-277-8004 **E-mail:** kunm@unm.edu

New York

CKON 97.3 FM	P. O. Box 140 Rooseveltown, NY 13683	**Phone**: 518-358-3426 **Fax**: 613-575-2566 **e-mail**:ckon@cnwl.igs.net

North Dakota

KABU 90.7 FM	C/O Cankdeska Cikana Community College PO Box 269 Fort Totten, ND 58335	**Phone**: 701-766-1995 **Fax**: 701-766-4077
KEYA 88.5 FM	Old Hospital Road PO Box 190 Belcourt, ND 58316	**Phone:** 701-477-5686 **Fax:** 701-477-3252 **E-Mail:** keya@utma.com
KMHA 91.3 FM	Ft. Berthold Communications Enterprise HCR 3, P.O.BOX 1 New Town, ND 58763	**Phone**: 701-627-3333 **Fax**: 701-627-4212 **E-Mail:** kmha_fm@restel.net

Ohio

WYSO 91.3 FM	Antioch University 795 Livermore Street Yellow Springs, OH 45387	**Phone:** 513-767-6420 **Fax:** 513-767-6961 **E-Mail:** wyso@antioch-college.edu

Oklahoma

KGOU 106.3 FM **KROU** 105.7 FM	University of Oklahoma 780 Van Fleet Oval, Room 339 Norman, OK 73019	**Phone:** 405-325-3388 **Fax:** 405-325-7129 **E-Mail:** kholp@ou.edu

Oregon
KWSO
91.9 FM

PO Box 489
Warm Springs, OR 97762

Phone: 541-553-1968
Fax: 541-553-3348

South Dakota
KILI
90.1 FM

PO Box 150
Porcupine, SD 57772

Phone: 605-867-5002
Fax: 605-867-5634
E-Mail: lakotaco@gwtc.net

KINI
96.1 FM

P.O. Box 419
St. Francis, SD 57572

Phone: 605-747-2291
Fax: 605-747-5791
E-Mail: KINIFM@gwtc.net

KLND
89.5 FM

Seventh Generation Media
Services
HC 61, Box 1
McLaughlin, SD 57642

Phone: 605-823-4661
Fax: 605-823-4660
E-Mail: klnd@westriv.com

KSWS
89.3 FM

PO Box 142
Sisseton, SD 57262

Phone: 605-698-7972
Fax: 605-698-7897

Washington
KOTY
1490 AM

Yakama Indian Nation
Radio Project
P.O. Box 151
Toppenish, WA

Phone (main): 509-865-5362
Phone (studio): 509-865-3900

KSFC
89.3 FM

Spokane Public Radio, Inc.
2319 N. Monroe Street
Spokane, WA 99205

Phone: 509-328-5729
Fax: 509-328-5764
E-mail: dnadvorn@kpbx.org

Wisconsin
WOJB
88.9 FM

RR 2 Box 2788
Hayward, WI 54843

Phone: 715-634-2100
E-mail: wojbfm@aol.com

WYMS
89 FM

5225 W Vliet St
Milwaukee, WI 53208

Phone:414-475-8362
Fax: 414-475-8362
E-mail: rdobrick@aol.com

Canada
CKMR
88.1 FM

Box 89
Morley, AB TOL 1NO

Phone: 403-881-2021
Fax: 403-881-2027

COKI
103.1 FM

Box 1490
Siksika, AB TOJ 3WO

Phone: 403-264-7250, ext. 5340
Fax: 403-734-5497
E-mail:
shanebreaker@hotmail.com

CIUT
89.5 FM

Toronto, ON

Phone: 416-978-0909 ext 201
E-mail: n_perera@ciut.fm

Index

A

B

C

140

N

O

P

R

S

T

U

V

W

X

Y

Z

Printed in the United States
17918LVS00001B/91